HOSPITALITY AND TOURISM MARKETING

HOSPITALITY
AND
TOURISM MARKETING

SUNIL SHARMA

AKANSHA PUBLISHING HOUSE
NEW DELHI

AKANSHA PUBLISHING HOUSE
R 37-B, Vani Vihar, Uttam Nagar
New Delhi-110059
Email: ektabooks@yahoo.com

Showroom
4649/21B, Ansari Road
Darya Ganj
New Delhi - 110 002
Ph.: 23269193 / 9811582579

Hospitality and Tourism Marketing

First Edition 2005
ISBN 81-8370-017-9

PRINTED IN INDIA

Published by M.P. Misra for Akansha Publishing House, New Delhi and
Printed at : **Mehra Offset Press, New Delhi.**

Contents

Preface

Marketing is a social and managerial process by which individuals and groups obtain what they need and want through creating and exchanging products and value with others. Hospitality marketing is part of a larger industry known as travel and tourism. It includes processes such as purchasing food and restaurant supplies, suggesting fries to go with that burger, doing what it takes to satisfy the customer and the company and advertising and promoting special room rates to increase business.

The hospitality industry blends the marketing of goods and services in a unique way. Customer satisfaction leading to profit is the central goal of hospitality and tourism marketing. Not only do travellers seek a clean and comfortable room, they also want someone to keep it that way. Not only do restaurant customers want quality food, they want someone to prepare and serve it well. Hotels, restaurants, and other businesses involved in travel and tourism balance basic marketing elements to meet the needs of customers while making a reasonable profit at the same time.

Attracting and pleasing the customer is the prime motive of hospitality marketing. A strong economy, a mobile population, and more disposable income have increased profit potential for the hotel and motel industry. These trends have also increased the competition to secure hotel and motel guests. To be successful, the hospitality industry must maintain high standards to meet the expectations of consumers and ensure repeat business, and keep up with the latest trends for survival.

The present book is a comprehensive core marketing text specifically geared for hospitality students and professionals. It covers the major principles of marketing with a practical, applications oriented approach. The latest developments in this rapidly changing field with updated information, new case histories, and fresh examples drawn from a broad range of hospitality operations are also included. This book will be an important career-building guide in the hands of future hospitality professionals.

Editor

1

Basics of Marketing

Marketing is a well-known word, it is often misused or misunderstood. Marketing has changed a great deal over the past 20 years. Some businesses still do not use marketing effectively. Marketing is a rather large category covering a number of different activities that provides broad benefits when used effectively. There are differences between effective and ineffective marketing.

Marketing is now an important activity essential not only to the success of manufacturers and retailers, but also to government agencies, hospitals, law offices, schools, and churches. Marketing has a number of major functions with numerous examples performed by almost every business. Successful businesses develop an approach to marketing planning that responds to the needs of customers so that customers will be satisfied with the products and services they purchase.

Marketing is one of the most visible business activities around us. We do not often see products being manufactured, accountants maintaining the financial records of a business, or human resources managers hiring and training personnel. But we can see marketing every day. Marketing includes advertisements on the radio, products being transported by truck, and marketing researchers in shopping malls. We are involved in marketing. We make marketing decisions regularly. We assist routinely in the effective marketing of products and services.

Marketing activities are involved when we select the products or services we intend to purchase. We are involved in marketing activities when we decide to use cash or a credit card and when we pay for the delivery of a bulky product to our home. By studying marketing, we will learn how businesses use marketing to increase their effectiveness and the profits they make. We will also improve our personal marketing skills. Those skills are useful to us as a consumer as we make better purchasing decisions. Marketing skills are used as an application for college. We can use marketing skills when we interview with a potential employer.

Marketing skills are used also when we serve as a leader of an organization. And they are the skills needed for many exciting and wellpaying careers in the business world. Every business today is involved in marketing. Over four million firms in the United States have marketing as their primary business activity. Examples of those businesses are advertising agencies, real estate offices,marketing research businesses,finance companies,travel agencies,and retail stores. Most large businesses have marketing departments employing many types of marketing specialists. Even small companies are finding they need to employ people who understand marketing and are able to complete a number of marketing activities. There are many types of marketing jobs ranging from selling to inventory management.

Careers in advertising, sales promotion, customer service, credit, insurance, transportation, and research require preparation in marketing. Marketers work for manufacturers, law offices, hospitals, museums,professional sports teams, and symphonies. There are marketing jobs available as we begin our career. These jobs include retail clerk, bank teller, stock person, telemarketing interviewer, and delivery person. Marketing positions can be among the highest paid jobs in most companies. Because of the change and growth that has occurred in marketing, many people view it as the most diverse and exciting career area of the 21st century. When many people hear the word marketing they only think of advertising and selling. However, many marketing activities need to be completed before a product or service is ever ready to be advertised and sold.

Marketing Activities

Marketing activities can be grouped into seven functions. These functions are, Product/Service Management, Distribution, Selling, Marketing-Information Management, Financing, Pricing, and Promotion.

Product/Service: Management Assisting in the design and development of products and services that will meet the needs of prospective customers.

Distribution: Determining the best methods and procedures to be used so prospective customers are able to locate, obtain, and use the products and services of an organization.

Selling: Direct, personal communications with prospective customers in order to assess needs and satisfy those needs with appropriate products and services.

Marketing-Information: Management Obtaining, managing, and using market information to improve decision making and the performance of marketing activities.

Financing: Budgeting for marketing activities, obtaining the necessary financing, and providing financial assistance to customers to assist them with purchasing the organization's products and services.

Pricing: Establishing and communicating the value of products and services to prospective customers.

Promotion: Communicating information to prospective customers through advertising and other promotional methods to encourage them to purchase the organization's products and services. Each of these functions occurs every time a product or service is developed and sold. The performance of the activities described in the functions is the responsibility of marketers. So we can see that marketing is a very complex part of business and is very important to the success of businesses and to the satisfaction of customers.

We can identify the marketing functions being performed by companies as they develop new products, improve marketing procedures, and respond to customer needs. We can find examples of these functions in hundreds of different forms. Sony used product/service management to develop the Video Walkman, which combines a 3-inch television with an 8-mm videocassette recorder. Hertz uses a unique distribution strategy as a part its car rental service. Hertz will park a car at the exit of an airport terminal with the engine running, heated in the winter or cooled in the summer, and with all paperwork completed for selected customers to speed their departure from the airport.

Many professional firms are recognizing the importance of personal selling to the success of their practices. Selected executives in law offices, accounting firms, and banks are completing professional sales training in order to effectively develop new clients for the businesses. The electronic scanners used at checkouts of supermarkets provide information on purchases so managers can instantly determine what is being purchased in order to keep the best assortment of products available for customers. This is an example of the use of marketing-information management. Major automobile manufacturers, such as General Motors, demonstrate the financing function when they maintain their own financing organizations (like GMAC) to make loans to consumers available at the automobile dealerships.

A bakery manager notices that customers aren't purchasing pastries, cookies, and other snacks because they are too expensive. As part of the pricing function, she lowers the prices and places a sign in the front window advertising them. Businesses selling expensive products such as oceanfront condominiums prepare high-quality videotapes, which provide information and promote products using audio and video messages. The videotapes are sent to carefully selected customers to interest them in purchasing a condominium through a unique type of promotion.

Because of the many functions and activities that are part of marketing,it is not easy to develop a definition of marketing that effectively describes it. Marketing has changed in recent years and continues to change. A simple definition was presented in a 1960 book of marketing terms published by the American Marketing Association. Marketing was described as "the performance of business activities that direct the flow of goods and services from producer to consumer or user. " As marketing developed and was applied in a broad set of businesses and organizations, definitions became more complex. Marketing now includes customer research and product development activities.

It applies to nonprofit businesses and to organizations not considered businesses (churches, sororities and fraternities, schools, and libraries). Not only is marketing used for products and services, but for individuals (political candidates, artists, sports stars), and even to promote ideas (stop smoking, recycling, stay in school). The most recent definition of marketing, accepted by the American Marketing Association in 1985, is very long and complex, but it communicates how marketing has changed over the years. It defines marketing as the process of planning and executing the conception, pricing, promotion, and distribution of ideas, goods, and services to create exchanges that satisfy individual and organizational objectives.

Because marketing can be applied in very different ways in various businesses and organizations,and because marketing needs to be easily understood, the following simplified definition describes the value marketing offers to those who use it well. Marketing is the creation and maintenance of satisfying exchange relationships. We need to carefully consider all parts of this definition in order to understand marketing. Creation suggests that marketing is involved from the very beginning as products and services are being developed. Maintenance means that marketing must continue to be used as long as a business or organization is operating. Satisfaction of both the business and the customer is an important goal of marketing. When products or services are exchanged, the needs of everyone involved must be met as well as possible. Marketing is needed by, but not limited to, businesses that are selling products and services.

Necessity of Marketing

Ever since the first products were exchanged, there has been a need for marketing. In the past, marketing was viewed as a simple set of activities that would help a business sell its products to more customers. The very first businesses developed marketing to improve exchanges. Business managers know that marketing must be carefully planned. It must be coordinated with other business activities. The approach to managing marketing activities changes as businesses and other organizations implement the marketing concept.

Marketing is an important part of business. Some people believe that if a business offers a good product, marketing is not necessary. However, if the customer does not know about the product, does not know where to purchase it, is unable to get to the place where it is sold, cannot afford the price of the product, or does not believe the product is a good value, the product will not be purchased. Marketing is required to provide a variety of activities or services so the customer will be able to purchase the product.

Marketing cannot be successful if the product is not what the customer wants or is a poor quality product. While a customer may be encouraged to buy a product through advertising, selling, or a low price, the product must be seen as satisfying a need of the customer. If the customer decides to buy the product, and it does not work the way the customer was led to believe, if it is of poor quality, or if it has a defect, the customer will likely return the product for a refund. Even if the customer does not return a product that was not satisfying, it is unlikely the customer will buy the same product again. Businesses and other organizations use effective marketing to provide satisfying exchanges of products and services with customers. The ways marketing is used have changed over the years, but the need for marketing has not.

Development of Business

There have been times in history when people were self-sufficient. Being selfsufficient means we do not rely on others for the things needed in order to survive. People were able to find or produce the food and materials needed for themselves and their families. That type of lifestyle required very hard work and was very risky. Self-sufficient people had to have good hunting, fishing, or farming skills to obtain needed food as well as the capability of developing shelter, clothing, and other necessities. Often it was not possible to obtain everything needed to survive because of poor weather, competition with other people, sickness, or lack of skill.

Some people who found they were not successful at being self-sufficient tried to find other ways to survive. They saw that often, when they did not have certain things they needed,other people had those things. If each person had something that the other person valued, they were able to exchange, so each would be better off than before. Exchanging products or services with others by agreeing on their values is known as bartering. A system of bartering was developed so people could exchange with others to obtain the things they needed.

For example,in an early bartering system, someone who was a good hunter but was not able to grow grain might exchange products with another person who had extra grain but needed meat. People who had developed skills in weaving cloth might barter with people who raised animals. Exchanging products through bartering was one of the first examples of marketing. Bartering still takes place today on a limited scale, and is even taxed by the IRS.

People discovered that they had particular interests or skills in certain kinds of work, while they were not as good at or were uninterested in other types of work. If they concentrated on the work they did well, they were able to accomplish much more than if they tried to do a variety of things. Concentrating on one or a few related activities so that they can be done well is known as specialization of labor. Specialization of labor made it possible for people to produce larger quantities of a single product than if they were attempting to produce many different products. Therefore, more of that product would be available to exchange with other people.

As specialization of labor became more common and a greater variety and quantity of products were available, it was not always possible to barter. Not all people needed the products of others, and it was not always possible to reach agreement on what products were worth so that they could be exchanged directly. To assist with the exchange process, a money system was developed. A money system established the use of currency as a recognized medium of exchange. With money, people could obtain products even if they did not always have products on hand to exchange.

Those with products to sell could do so for money, which could then be used for future purchases. The development of a money system is another example of marketing.

With many people producing more types of products and with people having money to purchase the items they needed, the demand for products increased. It was a difficult process to locate and accumulate all of the products people wanted and needed. A great deal of time was spent traveling to sell and purchase products. To solve that problem, central markets were developed. A central market is a location where people bring products to be conveniently exchanged. Central markets were often located at places where many people traveled, such as where rivers or roads met.

Towns and cities developed at those locations and became centers of trade. People brought the products they wanted to sell to the markets. Those people needing to obtain products would also travel to the market to make purchases. Developing locations where products could be bought and sold was another step in the development of marketing.

Other Marketing Activities

As central markets expanded, other types of business services were created to make exchanges easier. It was not always possible for sellers and buyers to travel to the markets at the same time. Therefore, businesses were formed to purchase products from producers and hold them for sale to purchasers. Other businesses were started to loan money to buyers or sellers, to help with transportation of products, or to locate products that were not available in the market but that customers wanted. Each of those activities resulted in the development of another marketing activity and made the exchange process more effective for those who produced products and for those who purchased and consumed the products.

Functions of Business

The previous examples have illustrated how marketing developed to improve the exchange of products between producers and consumers. It is clear that marketing is an important part of business and that businesses cannot be effective without marketing. But marketing cannot be successful alone. A number of other activities are important to businesses.

Production

The primary reason for a business to exist is to provide products or services to consumers and to earn a profit. The production function creates or obtains products or services for sale. Think of the variety of products and services available from businesses and we can see that production can take various forms.

Raw Materials: Production includes obtaining raw materials for sale to customers. Mining, logging, drilling for oil, and similar activities are examples of this type of production.

Processing: Other businesses take raw materials and change their form through processing so they can be used in the production of other products or in the operation of businesses or equipment. Examples include oil refining and the production of steel, paper,plastics, food products, and so forth. A third example of production is agriculture, where food and other materials are grown for consumption or for processing into a variety of products. Manufacturing businesses are also involved in production. Those businesses use raw materials and other resources to produce products for sale to consumers or to other businesses. Most of the products consumed by our friends, our family, and businesses have been produced by manufacturers.

Services : The development of services is also an example of the production function. While a physical product is not provided to the customer, offering a service such as preparing tax returns, cutting hair, providing lawn maintenance services, or performing a concert meets customer needs in the same way as making consumable products. Finally, some businesses do not produce or manufacture products but accumulate products for resale to customers. Offering products produced or manufactured by others for sale to customers is known as merchandising. Retailers and wholesalers are examples of merchandising businesses. While merchandising is not production, it makes products available for sale in those businesses in the same way that production and manufacturing do for other businesses.

Operations

The ongoing activities designed to support the primary function of a business and to keep a business operating efficiently are known as operations. Many things must occur for a business to successfully produce and market products and services. Buildings and equipment must be operated, maintained, and repaired. Products must be obtained, transported, stored, and protected. Paperwork must be completed. Customer questions must be answered and customer services provided. The way operations are completed often means the difference between profit or loss for a business.

Accounting and finance

Businesses are very complex with a variety of activities occurring at the same time. A large amount of money is handled by most businesses in many forms including cash, checks, and credit. The accounting and finance function plans and manages financial resources and maintains records and information related to businesses' finances. Finance begins by determining the amount of capital needed for the business and where that capital will be obtained.

Budgets must be developed,watched carefully, and updated. Most businesses must regularly borrow money for major purchases as well as for some day-to-day operations. Determining sources for borrowing,interest rates, and loan payback schedules are important responsibilities of accounting and finance personnel. Without careful record keeping and an understanding of the financial situation,managers will be unable to plan the activities of the business. The accounting and finance function provides that type of information and assistance in the business.

Management and adminisitration

Even the smallest businesses require that considerable time be spent in planning and organizing activities. Someone must determine what the business will do, how it can best meet the needs of customers, and how to respond to competitors' actions. Problem-solving, managing the work of employees, and evaluating the activities of the business are ongoing responsibilities of managers. The management and administration function involves developing, implementing, and evaluating the plans and activities of a business. Managers are responsible for everything that occurs in the business including the work of the employees. They must develop objectives and plans,make sure the appropriate resources are available, be responsible for buildings and equipment, and assign responsibilities to others. Managers are held responsible for the performance of the company, including whether or not it is profitable.

Marketing

Marketing is also an important function of business. All businesses need to complete a variety of activities in order to make their products and services available to consumers and to ensure that effective exchanges occur. Those activities are known as marketing.

Coordination

Each of the functions of business is dependent on the other functions if the business is to be effective. Products can be produced, but if the company is not operated or managed effectively, if adequate records are not maintained, or if marketing is not successful, the products will not be sold at a profit. In the same way, operations, management, and administration are used to coordinate the work of the business. Finance and accounting provide information to the other parts of the business to ensure that a profit is possible. Some organizations have not been successful in coordinating the business functions.

The various functions operated independently and often competed with each other. Products were produced that could not be sold. Marketing activities were planned with little attention to their costs. Managers concentrated on specific activities of the business without considering if their decisions would have negative effects on other functions. The result was that the quality of products and customer service declined while prices increased. Customers became unhappy when they found that products were declining in quality, they could not get the level of service they expected, or prices were increasing rapidly. Competitors who were better organized were able to take advantage of those situations.

Most businesses recognize that they must carefully coordinate the functions and activities if they are going to satisfy their customers and make a profit. Managers and employees are trained to work together. A great deal of planning is done to determine how activities should be organized.

Marketing Concept

Marketing was not always an important part of business. Indeed,marketing was not even a term used in business until the last half of the twentieth century. In the early part of that century, businesses were concerned about producing products that customers needed and were able to afford. Major efforts that could be considered marketing were directed at getting the products to customers. There were not many choices of transportation methods, and roads and highways were not well developed. The primary way to sell more products was to be able to deliver them to a larger number of customers. As consumers increased their standard of living and had more money to spend, the demand for newer and better products increased.

Demand was usually greater than the available supply of products. Business people concentrated on production and seldom had to worry a great deal about marketing. Customers were often eager to buy new products and would seek out the manufacturer when they heard of a product they wanted. Over time production processes improved, there was more competition among producers and manufacturers,and consumers had more choices of products and services available. Therefore, businesses had to compete with each other to get customers to buy their products. Businesses began to increase their attention to basic marketing activities,such as advertising and selling, to convince customers that their products were superior to those of competitors.

Customer Needs

As it became more and more difficult and expensive for businesses to sell their products, some business people began to realize an important fact. Businesses could no longer be successful by just producing more products or by increasing the amount of advertising and selling efforts for the products. They had to produce products that customers wanted. The most successful businesses were the ones that considered customers' needs and worked to satisfy those needs as they produced and marketed their products and services. That philosophy of business is now known as the marketing concept.

The marketing concept is using the needs of customers as the primary focus during the planning, production, distribution, and promotion of a product or service. Using the marketing concept is not as easy as it might sound. Three activities must be accomplished by businesses if they want to use it successfully. These are;

— First, the business must be able to identify what will satisfy customers' needs.

— Second,the business must be able to develop and market products or services that customers consider to be better than other choices.

— Third,the business must be able to operate profitably.

Many businesses are successfully identifying and responding to needs of customers. Fast food restaurants provide breakfast menus and late night hours in order to have their products available when customers want them. Many banks provide services so customers can pay bills, transfer money,and check account balances by using a telephone or a personal computer. Hospitals offer wellness programs,weight loss clinics, and fitness centers to attract clients and broaden their image. Colleges offer courses to area high school students to allow college credits to be earned prior to graduation and to interest students in enrolling full time at the college.

Businesses that do not use the marketing concept are more concerned about producing products than understanding customer needs. Once products are developed, they rely on marketing activities to try to sell those products. Some automobile manufacturers have some difficulty to selling their cars. In some cases the difficulty results because they are not producing the type, style, or quality of cars customers want. The companies then have to use extensive advertising, price reductions, rebates, and pressure selling to convince customers to buy a product that is not really what the customers prefer. Retail stores sometimes buy products that they believe will sell, but then see that customers are not willing to buy them.

The stores then have to cut prices, increase advertising, use special displays, and other strategies to convince customers to buy the products. The extra expenses of marketing products that customers may not have a strong interest in buying can lead to reductions in profit or even losses for the business. Additionally, after purchasing the product, the customer may decide it is not what was wanted and return the product to the business or become very unhappy with both the product and the company that sold it. The customer may be reluctant to buy from that company in the future and may express dissatisfaction to prospective customers, resulting in reduced sales for the company.

Companies that believe in the marketing concept operate differently than those who do not. Businesses using the marketing concept follow a two-step process.

Identify the market: The first step is to identify the market they want to serve. A market refers to the description of the prospective customers a business wants to serve and the location of those customers. An example of a market for a bicycle manufacturer may be people who ride bicycles for health and fitness in the mountains. A potential market for a sports arena may be teenagers within 80 miles of the arena who attend concerts more than two times a year.

Develop a marketing mix: The second step is to develop a marketing mix that will meet the needs of the market and that the business can provide profitably. A marketing mix is the blending of four marketing elements by the business.

The bicycle manufacturer may decide to offer a mountain bike with three choices of frames and tires. They can sell through a selected group of bicycle shops in resort towns in Colorado,Wyoming, Utah, and New Mexico. The price can range from $280-$550. It can be promoted by advertising in two fitness magazines, a cable sports channel, and by salespeople in the bicycle shops.

The sports arena manager could choose a marketing mix for concerts that includes groups that have albums in the top 40 of the pop/rock charts, scheduled on Saturday or Sunday evenings, priced at $60 for reserved seating and $32 for open seating, and promoted on the three area FM radio stations with the highest audience ratings for listeners age 15-25. Basic definitions of each mix element are as follows.

— Product is anything offered to a market by the business to satisfy needs, including physical products, services, and ideas.

— Distribution or place includes the locations and methods used to make the product available to customers.

— Price is the actual amount that customers pay and the methods of increasing the value of the product to the customers.

— Promotion includes the methods and information communicated to customers to encourage purchases and increase their satisfaction.

While each of the definitions is written to describe marketing of products by a business, the mix elements are also part of services and ideas. Non-business organizations and even individuals can effectively develop marketing mixes. The strategies of effective marketing that we will be learning have very broad applications.

Changing Roles Marketing

While marketing is necessary in all exchanges, businesses

have not always believed marketing was important. They expected customers to take most of the responsibility for completing marketing activities. Only recently have many business people realized the value of effective marketing. There are several changes in the role that marketing has played in U. S. businesses during the past century.

Production emphasis

In the early years of the last century, production processes were very simple and few product choices were available. People had limited money to spend on products and much of their purchasing was for basic necessities. Transportation systems were not well developed so it was difficult to get products from where they were manufactured to the many people throughout the United States. In that environment, businesses believed that if they could produce products, they would be able to sell them. So they concentrated on developing new products and improving the process of production. The only real marketing effort was devoted to distribution,moving products from the producer to the customer.

Sales emphasis

During the 1930s and into the 1940s, businesses became more effective at producing products. Efficient methods of producing large numbers of products at a low cost, such as assembly lines,were used. Transportation systems improved including the use of trains, boats, and trucks, making it easier to get products to more customers. At the same time, the standard of living of many Americans was improving, giving them money to spend on more products. These changes resulted in increased competition among businesses. They could no longer rely on customers buying their products just because they were able to get the products to the customers. Companies began to rely on salespeople to represent their products. The salespeople would attempt to convince customers that their company's products were better than the products of competitors.

Marketing department emphasis

The sales emphasis continued on until well into the 1950s for many businesses and well beyond that time for others. Then after World War II, the U. S. economy expanded rapidly and wage levels increased for consumers as their hours of work declined. Consumers had more money to spend and more time to enjoy the use of many products. Companies increasingly found that consumers were not easily convinced to purchase products when they had many choices available to them. Therefore, businesses had to find different ways to be sure that consumers purchased their products.

Companies began to develop marketing departments that were responsible for developing those new methods. One of the first efforts of the new marketing department was to expand the use of advertising. Advertising had an important role of informing consumers about a company's products, the reasons to buy the products, and where they could be located. New methods of getting products to customers were developed including catalog sales through the mail and even the use of airplanes to move some products very rapidly.

Products were distributed extensively through many retail stores. Customers were offered credit to make purchases more affordable. As companies worked to find additional methods to encourage customers to buy, the marketing department became an important part of the business.

Marketing Concept emphasis

The marketing department emphasis showed that

marketing could be a very important tool for businesses. A number of activities were now available that had not been used in the past. However, just because more activities were used,companies were not always more successful. It was discovered that marketing was becoming quite expensive. Also, since the goal of the marketing department was to sell the products of the company,marketers began to misuse marketing activities. These unethical activities sometimes resulted in sales, but also led to customer complaints.

Examples included high-pressure sales, misleading advertising, and customer services that were not provided as promised. These earlier actions help explain why some people have a negative attitude toward sales people and advertisements. Marketers also discovered that no matter how hard they tried, there were products that customers did not want to buy. If customers did not believe the product would satisfy their needs, marketing was not effective.

Yet marketers were not involved in developing the company's products. In the 1970s, some companies began to realize they could be more successful if they listened to consumers and considered customer needs as they developed products and services. The marketing concept uses the needs of customers as the primary focus during the planning, production, distribution, and promotion of a product or service.

When the marketing concept was adopted, marketing became more than the work of one department. It was now a major part of the business. Marketing personnel worked closely with people in other parts of the company. Activities were completed with customer satisfaction in mind.

By coordinating the efforts of the departments in the company and by focusing on satisfying customers' needs, companies were able to develop and market products that customers wanted and that could be sold at a profit. Those companies were using the marketing concept. Since its first use in the 1970s, the marketing concept has been proven as an effective method and is now used by the majority of businesses and by other organizations.

Marketing is very different today than it was even just fifteen or twenty years ago. If we look back over the history of business, we can see that marketing has played a role in even the simplest early businesses. But business people have not recognized the full value of marketing as a business tool until recently.

The role of marketing in business has changed along with the definition. Previously, marketing was seen as a tool to help the business sell its products and services. It was not needed if sales were high. Today, business people see that marketing contributes in several important ways to the business. It provides information about customers and their needs through market research, which helps businesses plan more effectively.

Marketing provides many ways to serve customers better including distribution, pricing, credit, and customer services. Marketing can increase customer satisfaction by solving customer problems. Finally, marketing can help the business be more profitable by coordinating activities and controlling costs.

Because of the successful use of marketing in businesses, other organizations now look to marketing for help. Libraries, churches, government agencies, community organizations, and the military are using marketing activities. Some use marketing very well while others do not understand marketing. They may view marketing as advertising or selling only and not as a way of satisfying their customer or client needs. We can evaluate organizations to determine if they understand the value of marketing. If they rely on promotion with brochures,advertisements,and public service announcements,they probably view marketing as a way to convince consumers of the value of their organization.

Without research to help them understand their clients, they are not able to respond to the clients' needs. If they use marketing to determine what products and services to offer,where to make them available,how to help consumers determine the value of their services, and to communicate effectively with those consumers, they have adopted the marketing concept. The marketing concept works just as well for organizations as it does for businesses.

Marketing managers are responsible for a large number and variety of activities. They must work with many people inside and outside of a company. Marketing managers are ultimately responsible for a large part of the company's budget. People involved in marketing need information about customers, competitors, and market conditions. This information helps marketers make decisions that will result in sales and profits for the business. Marketers have varied amounts of experience and education. Marketing is an exciting and challenging career area. If we are interested in marketing we must be willing to develop the needed knowledge and skills. Marketing offers many opportunities for our future.

Effects of Marketing

Marketing is responsible for helping businesses find markets for their products and services and sell them profitably. But many people question the value of marketing. Some see it as adding to the cost of products. Others believe it causes people to buy things they otherwise would not want or need. Still others suggest that if businesses produce quality products and services, then there is no need for marketing. It is important to determine if marketing plays a positive or a negative role.

Manufacturers developing a new brand of toothpaste will make better decisions if they are aware of what consumers like and dislike about the current brand used.

The manager of a clothing store will want to know what consumers are expecting in terms of styles and prices before purchasing new items for sale. Marketing helps a business satisfy customer wants and needs. This means that customers are more likely to be loyal and continue to purchase from the business. Marketing also helps the business make better decisions about what to sell and how to sell it. Therefore, the business is more likely to operate efficiently. So, effective marketing is important to businesses.

Because marketing improves exchanges between businesses and consumers, individuals benefit from marketing. While many people do not easily recognize those benefits, those who understand marketing can provide examples of its value. Consider going to a supermarket to purchase supplies for a party. If the store is conveniently located, we will not have to worry about how we will get to and from the store. We want the store to stock our favorite brands of decorations, drinks, and snacks. There should be an adequate supply of the items we need. When we get into the store, the products should be easy to locate. The prices should be clearly marked and affordable. A store employee should be able to answer our questions and help to check out and bag our purchases. The store should allow us to pay for our purchases with cash, check, credit, or debit card.

Marketing provides other contributions to individuals that may not be as obvious. Because marketing is continually determining what consumers like and dislike and what needs are not satisfied, improvements are made to products and services and new products are developed. As a result of marketing activities, more products are available to meet the needs of more customers. This results in higher sales volume. The increase in sales allows businesses to produce products more efficiently and costs can actually decline.

The first personal computers were very basic and not very powerful, but cost several thousand dollars. Today's personal computers are hundreds of times more powerful, have many features to make them easy to use, and can be purchased for less than $1,000. This is possible because of improved technology and marketing.

Another contribution of marketing to individuals is a vast area of employment. Between one-fourth and one-third of all jobs in the United States are marketing jobs or have marketing as a major job responsibility. Salespeople, customer service representatives,warehouse managers, inventory specialists, marketing research personnel, and many others have interesting, financially rewarding careers because of marketing.

Finally, marketing skills are valuable to people who are not directly employed in marketing. By understanding the marketing process and using the marketing concept, we will be able to accomplish a number of our goals. Marketing skills can help us to get elected to an office in a club, prepare for a job or for college, plan a fund-raising activity for an organization, or start our own business. Through marketing, people can choose from a wide variety of products and services, find businesses that respond to their needs, have access to good jobs, and develop skills that help meet many personal goals. There are many positive effects of marketing for society.

New and Better Products

Marketing helps to identify and develop new and better products and services for consumers. Many of those products and services are beneficial to society in general. More efficient automobiles use less gasoline and cause less pollution. Biodegradable products reduce the growing need for landfill space. Products like airbags and motorcycle helmets reduce the number and severity of injuries from accidents. Marketing encourages businesses to provide products and services that consumers want. It also helps consumers make more effective decisions about what to purchase. As a result, the natural resources and raw materials of a country should be used more efficiently rather than being wasted on products consumers will not buy.

Improves the Standard of Living

Marketing improves the standard of living in a country. The standard of living is based on the products and services available to consumers, the amount of resources consumers have to obtain the products and services, and the quality of life for consumers. Countries that have well-developed marketing systems are able to make more and better products available to consumers. Those countries also have more jobs for their citizens and higher wage scales as a result of marketing.

Improving International Trade

Marketing has been particularly effective in improving international trade. International trade contributes many benefits to the participating countries and to the consumers in those countries. Think of the number of products we buy that were produced in another country. Just as the United States is a large consumer of foreign products, many businesses in this country sell products internationally. Without marketing, such benefits would not be possible.

Marketing activities are essential for international trade. Marketers help to determine where products can be sold and how to sell them in countries that may have very different business procedures,money systems, and buying practices. Methods of shipping and product handling must be identified or developed. Decisions about customer service must be made. Promotional methods appropriate for the people in each country or region have to be developed to ensure that customers understand the products and their benefits.

Marketing Criticisms

It would be easy to say that marketing has only positive results. That is not always the case. If not used appropriately, marketing can have negative effects. The misuse of marketing has led to some criticisms and has created a negative image for some marketing activities. Business people must take criticisms of marketing seriously. Those criticisms often represent the attitudes of many consumers. If consumers have a negative opinion about an important part of a business, it can affect whether they will be customers or not. Marketers and other business people need to study marketing practices to be sure they result in effective exchanges and customer satisfaction.

Unneeded Purchases

Through marketing,consumers have many choices of products available for them to purchase. Those products are readily available in many stores, are displayed in ways that make them easy to purchase, and are attractively packaged to attract attention. Advertising is used extensively to encourage people to consider specific brands of products.

Credit and special financing arrangements are available for most expensive products to make them seem more affordable. Marketing activities and the power of promotion can increase the sales of products and services. Businesses using the marketing concept should carefully consider the potential impact of marketing activities on consumers. While it might seem appropriate to use any tool that will result in more sales of a product, the long-term results of the sale should be considered as well. If a customer buys a product because of marketing rather than because the product is really needed, there is a good chance the customer will be dissatisfied.

Many consumers simply return the item, and expect a refund. The business not only has lost the sale, but now has a product that is worth much less than before and perhaps cannot be resold. Even if the consumers do not return the products, they are likely to be quite dissatisfied. That is particularly true if the product cost a great deal of money. The business is left with returned merchandise, a dissatisfied customer, and possibly a bad reputation among the customer's friends.

To respond to this criticism, business people must be very sensitive to the needs and experiences of customers. Products and services should be carefully matched to customers' needs. Products that do not sell should be evaluated to determine why customers do not want them. In that way, the business can make better purchasing decisions in the future in order to offer products and services that customers want.

Marketing should start with good products. If a product is not meeting customer needs, business people should avoid using marketing strategies such as promotion and price reductions to try to sell the product. This will often lead to dissatisfaction with the product and the business. Finally, the business must value long-term relationships with customers. One sale is not enough. The business will be successful when customers return again and again because they are satisfied with the business and believe the business is concerned about their needs.

Marketing Waste Money

The average cost of all marketing activities is about 50 percent of the price of products. For some products it is much higher and for others it is a very small percentage. Since many people think of marketing as only advertising and selling, they are upset when they believe those activities double the price of their purchases. In reality, selling and promotion are a small part of the cost of marketing-typically about 2-10 percent of the product's price. And effective selling and promotion do increase the value to the customer.

If a salesperson helps to select the best product for our needs rather than selling something we do not want, we have spent our money more effectively.

Advertising can provide product information so we can make the best choice, or inform we where a product can be purchased and when it is on sale. Advertising can even result in savings because of the information provided. Economists who study the impact of marketing activities on product prices have demonstrated that marketing actually results in lower prices in the long run. Because products can be sold to more customers, there is greater competition among businesses. When consumers have choices of products, they will usually buy those that are reasonably priced. That encourages businesses to keep prices as low as possible in order to be competitive. According to the economists, increased sales volume and competition result in lower prices for consumers.

Poor Quality Products

There are many examples of businesses that rely on marketing to sell poor quality products. Think of the used automobile with many defects that is sold only because the salesperson convinced the unsuspecting customer that the car was really in good condition. There are numerous tales of unsuspecting people buying land for a home based on information in a brochure or videotape, only to discover that the land is in a swamp or on the side of a steep mountain. Marketing is certainly misused in those situations to misrepresent poor products. On the other hand, consider whether or not a high-quality product needs marketing.

Without marketing, it would be the responsibility of the consumer to find out that the product exists and to gather information about it. The consumer would have to locate the product, pay cash for it, and transport it from where it was manufactured to where it was to be used. The customer would assume all of the risk in handling and moving the product. If it were damaged, the customer would be responsible. These examples and many others show that marketing is important even for quality products and services. Marketing activities must be performed in every exchange. If the business is not responsible for marketing, consumers will have to complete the activities themselves in order to purchase the product or service.

Marketing, if misused, can have negative results, however, marketing can help to solve important problems and contribute to social improvement. There are many examples of very positive results when marketing is used effectively.

There are many serious problems facing our society. Concerns about health care, crime levels, poverty, diseases, racism, education, unemployment, drug use, the environment, and teenage pregnancy all require the attention of many people if solutions are to be found. Marketing contributes to the solutions in several ways. Through communication, people are more aware of the problems and how they affect individuals and the country. Consider the number of times we have received information on using seat belts, recycling, the dangers of drugs and alcohol, and reasons to stay in school. Marketers have been responsible for developing the advertisements and public service announcements we have seen.

Marketing has encouraged people to eat low cholesterol products, quit smoking, contribute money to colleges, apply for scholarships, and support research into cures for diseases like AIDS and cancer. Marketing has encouraged people to vote and to avoid drinking and driving. We can think of many important social issues that are now receiving much attention because of effective marketing.

Products and services are not always available where they are most needed by consumers. For example, if there is a drought in one part of the country, farmers and ranchers in that area may not have enough hay and grain to feed their livestock. At the same time, there might be an excess supply in other areas. An effective distribution system can move the hay and grain quickly from one part of the country to another, matching supply and demand.

Social Responsibility

Protection of Consumer

Marketers cannot think only about selling products and making a profit. They must be aware of other effects of their activities. Marketing is a powerful tool that can have both positive and negative results. Marketers must be willing to pay attention to society's needs to determine how businesses can contribute to solutions. The trend today is a greater expectation for business to be socially responsible and to aid in solving the problems facing society. Concern about the consequences of actions on others is social responsibility.

Business people recognize that they must make decisions that consider factors beyond what their customers want and what is most profitable for the business. Most business people recognize their businesses cannot be successful in the long run if society is facing major problems. Increasing the social responsibility of businesses is occurring in three major ways. The growth of consumerism, government regulation, and improving business practices are each playing a role.

Consumerism

Consumerism is the organized actions of groups of consumers seeking to increase their influence on business practices. Consumers as individuals can have only a small influence on the activities of a business. However, when organized as a group of consumers, they have a much greater impact by speaking out, meeting with business people to recommend changes, and using the money they spend on purchases to influence decisions.

While consumers have always attempted to influence business practices, consumerism became an important influence on business practices in the 1960s when President John F. Kennedy presented the Consumer Bill of Rights. The Consumer Bill of Rights identified four basic rights that all consumers should expect: the right to adequate and accurate information, the right to safe products, the right to product choices, and the right to communicate their ideas and opinions to business and government. As a result of the attention focused on those rights, consumers have become very active in ensuring that their rights are protected. Some ways used to protect consumer rights are consumer education, consumer information, lobbying, and product boycotts.

Consumer groups develop materials and educational programs to be used in schools and in other places to help people become better consumers. We may have used some of those materials to learn how to use banking services, purchase insurance, and apply for loans. There are a number of consumer organizations that test products to determine whether they are safe and if they provide consumers with a good value for the price.

The organizations often publish the results in books,magazines, and on the Internet or have a telephone service so people can call for product information before making a purchase. Consumer lobbyists work with national and state legislators to develop laws to protect consumer rights. Finally, consumers have found they can influence business practices by the way they spend their money, their consumer vote. If a group of consumers is dissatisfied with the actions or products of a business they can organize a consumer boycott. A boycott is an organized effort to influence a company by refusing to purchase its products. Consumer groups also reinforce positive business practices by encouraging their members to purchase products from businesses that respond to consumer needs.

The United States government plays an active role in business practices. Many of the laws and regulations of government are designed to improve the social impact of business practices. Others are specifically developed to protect consumers. Most businesses recognize their responsibility to consumers and to society. If consumers are dissatisfied with the business'practices,they will soon stop buying the company's products. Social problems often lead to increased government regulation of business or increases in taxes to pay for programs designed to solve the problems. Businesses do not want increased regulation or taxes. Individual businesses and business organizations are working to improve business practices in several ways. Those ways include codes of ethics, self-regulation, and social action.

Codes of Ethics

A code of ethics is a statement of responsibilities for honest and proper conduct. Business people recognize that the inappropriate or illegal behavior of one firm can have a very negative effect on the whole industry. They attempt to influence that behavior by agreeing on standards of conduct. By agreeing to a code of ethics, the business people encourage responsible behavior. In some groups, the codes of ethics are enforced by penalties, established by the industry, that are applied to businesses that violate the standards.

Self-regulation

Individual businesses and groups of businesses in the same industry have developed procedures to respond to consumer problems and to encourage customers to work directly with the businesses to solve problems. Taking personal responsibility for actions is known as self-regulation. The Better Business Bureau is a consumer protection organization sponsored by businesses. The purpose of the Better Business Bureau is to gather information from consumers about problems, provide information about improper business practices so consumers can make better decisions, and attempt to solve problems between businesses and their customers.

Many businesses have consumer service departments that work to solve consumer problems and to provide consumers with information about the company and its products. The General Electric Answer Center offers a 24-hour-a-day, toll-free telephone service so customers can get information, register complaints, and make suggestions. Chrysler developed a Car Buyer's Bill of Rights and added the position of Vice President for Consumer Affairs to ensure those rights are protected. Some industries, such as homebuilders, developed procedures that consumers can use to resolve problems with a specific builder. Problems that cannot be resolved between the customer and the business are referred to an independent panel who can help determine a fair solution.

Business people are concerned about the world in which they live. Many are active in helping to solve some of society's serious problems. They use resources from their businesses to help. Members Only, a clothing manufacturer, spent more than $100 million on advertising messages directed at reducing drug abuse and increasing voter registration. More recently it directed its efforts toward alleviating the homeless problem. Nike committed about $50 million to a literacy program. McDonalds sponsors Ronald McDonald Houses for families with children who are hospitalized with serious illnesses. Each day we can see many examples of businesses that are concerned about their communities. They invest time and money to help the community and its people.

Business ethics have received a great deal of attention recently. Ethics is decisions and behavior based on honest and fair standards. Most business people behave ethically. However, the actions of a few people can cause customers to wonder if ethical behavior is really valued in business.

Consumers' Responsibility

Marketers deal directly with customers. They ask customers to spend money for products intended to satisfy needs and wants. Because of this relationship, marketers have a special responsibility to behave ethically. People place a high value on ethical business behavior. Business people are expected to be honest and fair in dealings with customers, employees, and other businesses. The American Marketing Association Code of Ethics describes specific responsibilities for marketers in the areas of product planning, promotion, pricing, distribution, and marketing research.

Each marketer is responsible for ethical behavior. Decisions and actions should be evaluated to determine if they are honest and fair. Sometimes there will appear to be conflicts in what is best for the business, for employees, for customers and competitors, and for society in general. Some people suggest the decision should be based on what is best for the most people. Others believe an action is right or wrong based on the effects on the people directly involved.

In some cases, it may appear there is no real harm in unethical behavior. If dishonesty results in a customer buying our product rather than our competitor's, or if we can conceal a mistake we made, we may believe that it does not matter. That is not the case. Marketers must remember that their emphasis must be on what is best for everyone involved in an exchange. Their actions usually affect many others, both inside and outside the business.

In other cases, unethical behavior has negative consequences for individuals and businesses. Improper marketing can harm customers. Society is hurt by businesses that have no concern for the products and services they sell or how or to whom they are marketed. Finally,many unethical business practices are also illegal. People have been fined and even imprisoned as a result of unethical actions. Some businesses are developing education programs and operating procedures to help employees understand how to make ethical decisions. Those businesses want to improve the ethical image of all businesses and ensure customers believe they will be treated fairly by every employee.

2

Market Analysis

A strong economy, a mobile population, and more disposable income have increased profit potential for the hotel and motel industry. These trends have also increased the competition to secure hotel and motel guests. Travelers have a wide array of choices for lodging. From metropolitan hotels with fine restaurants and personal service to discount motels offering clean, basic rooms and continental breakfast for a reasonable price, places for consumers to spend their dollars vary widely. Advertising campaigns use radio, television, newspaper, and now the Internet for slogans like "We'll leave the light on for you," and "Never underestimate the importance of a good night's rest," to stay in the minds of consumers. Attracting hotel guests takes more than a catchy slogan, though. First, the lodging establishment must determine a target market or a specific group of people who share similar characteristics as its hotel clientele.

Hotels may cater to repeat business travelers, vacationers and families in particular places, or transients, guests who visit an area or stay in a lodging property for only a few days. Each of these groups has different needs and desires, and makes decisions about how to spend dollars differently.

In order to compete for those dollars, a lodging establishment must know what its customers want. It can then determine what extras it will offer guests and what prices must be charged to pay for them. Most hotels and restaurants conduct marketing research to determine what customers expect. Hotel management pays close attention to demographics. Demographics are the characteristics of a target market such as age, income, gender, and level of education. These factors are directly related to choices that hotel management makes about pricing, amenities, and services.

Market conditions in your area have a significant impact on the profitability of your hotel or motel. The strength of the local lodging market affects how many rooms you can sell and the rates that you can charge. Developing a business plan for an existing business or conducting a feasibility study for a new venture requires a thorough analysis of market conditions.

Industry Trends

Studying national and regional industry trends will help you identify opportunities and threats that may affect your profitability. Relevant trends might include the growth in demand for overnight accommodations, changes in travellers' lodging needs, and new, innovative properties that are opening around the country.

The industry trends checklist provides a sample of topics you might want to study as part of your market analysis.

— Growth in Industry

  — Occupancy and Room Rates

  — Limited service vs. full service

  — Chain vs. independent

  — Industry sales outlook

— Market Demand

— Business travel preferences and trends

— Leisure travel preferences and trends

— Group travel preferences and trends

— Factors that motivate one to select hotel

— Market Supply

— Aging of existing lodging facilities

— New types of properties (all-suite, extended stay, "hard budget", etc.

— Growth in number of properties

— Financing for new properties

— Alternative lodging accommodations (i. e. bed & breakfast, other)

— Success and Failure Factors

— Service

— Facilities

— Amenities

— Pricing practices

— Reservation systems

— Property size

— Debt -to-sales and other statistics

— Legislative and Regulatory Issues

— Health Insurance

— Wage and hour requirements

— Americans with Disabilities Act (ADA)

Location

Location is a critical consideration because if affects your ability to draw customers. It is important that your location be visible, accessible, convenient and attractive to your market. Surrounding land uses are important for all types of lodging operations. Aesthetics of the area, noise, safety and other factors should be considered. How you evaluate your location will depend on the type of property you are operating or planning and the customers you hope you serve.

Commercial Locations

By location along major highways or in business or industrial districts, hotels and motels benefit from high visibility and proximity to generators of room night demand. Local colleges, hospitals, attractions, services and entertainment are examples of "room night" demand generators. Be sure to consider future growth patterns when analysing your site.

Resort Locations

Hotels and motels in resort areas generate most of their business form leisure travellers who see the lodging facility and surrounds area as their "destination. " Access and visibility, while important, are secondary to the quality of the facility, services, amenities, and nearby attractions. Different types of lodging operations will have different location requirements. Analyse your location using the factors listed on the following location checklist. Be sure to consider other location criteria to your particular hotel or motel. Following are the checklist of market analysis.

— Description of immediate area
    — Commercial profile
    — Adjacent land uses
    — Proposed developments
    — Safety
    — Availability of nearby services (food, fuel,

    shopping...)
  - Map of area (identify sources of demand, competition and other relevant landmarks)
- Proximity to demand generators
  - Business demand generators (industry, business, government, ...)
  - Colleges, hospitals and other institutions
  - Convention centers
  - Tourist attractions (museums, historical sites, recreation, ...)
- Traffic Volume
  - Highway/Street traffic counts
  - Traffic patterns
- Accessibility
  - Proximity to major streets and highways
  - Ease of entrance and exit
- Other Issues
  - Is the site large enough?
  - Social, political and environmental concerns
  - Area growth patterns

Local Market

In addition to having a good site, a lodging facility must be located in a market area that attracts overnight visitors. Following are the indicators of market area vitalities.

Business Community

Hotels and motels that primarily serve business travellers usually rely on the strength of the local business community. The size, stability and diversity of major local employers are important factors that should be researched. Plans for future business development should also be studied. Local planning officials and chambers of commerce are good sources for this information. Ask for information to help you understand trends over the past ten years and the future outlook.

Tourism Activity

Hotels and motels in resort areas typically rely on local attractions to bring in customers. Attractions can include both natural and man-made places of interest. Attraction operators may be able to provide you with estimates of attendance and data describing seasonality trends and place of customer origin.

Transportation Network Serving

An analysis of the transportation network serving the market area is also important. Existing highways and proposed highway improvements should be identified. Distances to feeder markets (where the guests originate) may be particularly important for resort hotels. Local economic and demographic trends should also be considered.

The following market area checklist includes information relevant to your operation. Use it to complete this part of your market analysis.

- — Business and Economic Characteristics
  - — Room tax collections
  - — Eating and drinking place sales
  - — Retail sales
  - — Employment (levels, types, major employers)
  - — Office/Industrial space occupied
  - — Business and plant closings

  - New businesses planned
- Tourism and Recreation Characteristics
  - Park visitation
  - Museum visitation
  - Casino visitation
  - Festivals and events visitation
  - Attractions visitation
  - Snowmobile trail usage
  - Boating activity
  - Hunting and fishing activity
  - New tourism attractions planned
- Transportation Factors
  - Distance from major cities
  - Traffic volume
  - Airport volume
  - Ferry volume
  - Passenger rail volume
- Other Market Characteristics
  - Population
  - Household income distribution
  - Local wage rates
  - Availability of labour
  - Types of labour available

Municipal room tax collections can provide you with a measure of the growth in lodging revenues during the past three to five years.

Competition

Probably the most important part of a lodging market analysis is the study of current and proposed competition. It is sometimes helpful to conduct interviews with the operators of other hotels nearby to learn about their operation and performance. An important part of your competition analysis is estimating the monthly and annual operation performance of each competitive property. Performance can be measured in terms of occupancy percent and average daily room rate.

Occupancy Percent = Number of Rooms Sold / Number of Rooms Available

Average daily room rate = Total Room Revenue / Number of Rooms Sold

In addition to occupancy and average room rates, each competitive operation should be carefully studied to determine its strengths, weaknesses and competitive position in the market area. Local planners and the development departments of hotel companies are usually aware of developments proposed for your community.

- Location
  - Proximity to sources of demand
  - Accessibility
  - Visibility
  - Surrounding neighbourhood
- Facility
  - Age
  - Exterior appearance and condition
  - Interior appearance and condition
  - Cleanliness
  - Signage
  - Types of rooms (suites, standard room,...)
  - Food and beverage outlets

    - Function rooms
    - Recreation (pool, fitness center, ...)
- Service
    - Quality of service
    - Extra services offered
- Information from Hotel/Motel Managers
    - Weekday vs. weekend demand patterns
    - Historical occupancy growth or decline
    - Monthly occupancy levels
    - Number of 100% occupancy days per month
    - Average room rate per month (after any discounts)
    - Major market segments served per month
    - Major sources of demand
- General Information
    - Number of rooms
    - Months open
    - Published rates
    - Franchise affiliation
    - Ratings in travel guides

Lodging Demand

Once you have analyzed your competition and their customers, you should carefully study what market segments of overnight guests visit your community. These market segments typically fall into four categories: business, leisure, group, and other.

Business

Business travellers represent a large portion of lodging

demand in many market areas. They include people travelling on business representing commercial, industrial and governmental organizations. Peak business demand is usually experienced Monday through Thursday nights. It is important to understand why business travellers are visiting the market area and how many room nights they generate. Reasons for visiting a particular area might include conducting business with a local company; calling on multiple businesses and stopping over between destinations. Interviews width local business representatives can be the most effective way to estimate how many room nights they might generate. Questions to ask include: type of visitors, frequency of visits, length of stay, where most visitors tend to stay and what rate range is acceptable.

Leisure

Leisure travellers may visit an area for a vacation, to attend sporting or social events, to shop, or to visit friends and relatives. They might be staying over simply because they are gravelling to other destinations. Leisure travellers may be individuals, couples, families, or small groups. Travellers visiting hospitals and universities are typically included in this market segment.

Leisure room demand is often seasonal. In larger, more urban market areas, leisure room demand may be limited to weekends, summer months and holiday periods. To measure the significance of leisure demand in your market area, interview the local visitor bureau, Chamber of Commerce and local event and attraction operators. Also, study variations in room rates by day of week and time of year. Higher rates usually indicate periods of higher occupancy. Finally, inspect local hotels and motels to determine if they have been designed to serve leisure travellers. Recreational facilities such as pools, fitness centers, tennis courts, snowmobile trails and other features may indicate the importance of leisure travellers to a particular property.

Group Meeting

The group market consists of both leisure and business travellers. Leisure groups include bus tours, school activities, athletic events, etc. Tour groups are often brought to an area for sightseeing and attending special events. Local attractions that appeal to leisure tour groups may have records of the numbers and names of tour operators who have visited their attractions. The National Tour Association and American Bus Association, among others, can provide information on tour activity. Business group meetings are typically associated with conferences, board meetings, training programs, seminars, trade shows, and other gatherings.

Often the sponsoring organization will be from the local area. Out-of-town organizations may use local meeting facilities because they often rotate the sites of their regional meetings. Information on the group meeting market can be obtained through state chapters of Meeting Planners International and the American Society of Association Executives. Your community's convention and visitor's bureau or chamber of commerce can usually provide a good estimate of local group meeting activity.

Other Travellers

Various lodging customers cannot be classified under the categories of business, leisure, or group. These travellers may include construction workers, truckers, utility crews and others. Activity at local truck stops, distribution centers, long term construction projects and other sources of demand could help you estimate the significance of this market segment.

Analysing Visitor Origin

Analysing visitor origin can be a complicated process. As these visitors may be gravelling great distances, it can be more difficult to acquire customer information than with a traditional analysis of local residents. Nonetheless, understanding these customers requires obtaining information about their places of origin, as well as data about their demographics and lifestyles. A technology called geographic information systems (GIS) can be used to solve these problems. Combining GIS with your customer address lists or chamber of commerce inquiry records, gives you the ability to profile tourism customers both geographically and demographically. Furthermore, GIS technology can use this information to search (prospect) for new potential customers in other communities that match your geographic or demographic criteria.

3

Tourism Marketing

Marketing is an essential part of running a business. New tourism businesses need to undertake at least some basic marketing initiatives to be successful. The best hotel, tour or attraction in the world will not succeed without a planned approach to marketing. The good news is that effective marketing does not need to cost a lot of money.

Tourism is a complex industry that involves a wide range of businesses working at different levels - from service stations and newsagents to hotels, motels, tour operators and travel agents.

Tourism is about providing experiences which involves a number of steps:

— People need to be motivated to travel

— People need to know what their holiday options are and what different destinations offer

— Bookings need to be made for accommodation, travel, tours etc. and

— Service providers (eg. tour, transport and accommodation operators etc.) need to deliver their product.

Each party in the chain contributes to the overall holiday experience of the customer. They form part of a network of wholesalers, retailers, and providers of tourism products and services that together deliver a complete travel package. If one party fails to deliver, the total travel experience of the customer could be ruined and reflect badly on all the other service providers, even if they did nothing wrong. Tourism is a 'big picture' business - understanding where the organisation fits into the network will help marketing managers to manage it successfully.

Market Segments

Tour products appeal to different types of people or markets, each with varying tastes and budgets. These include people wanting to stay in up-market resorts that pamper to their every need, to backpackers who are more interested in discovering the flora and fauna of the host country than luxury accommodation. The expectations of these two different markets are very different and the success of any tourism business will depend on knowing who their markets are and developing products that meet the needs of those markets.

Seasonality

Seasonal fluctuations have a major impact on tourism, eg. weather conditions, school holidays or the presence of a particular animal or feature at certain times. Periods of high demand are called 'peaks', periods of low demand are known as the 'off season', whilst the remainder are known as the 'shoulder' periods. Tourism businesses need to consider seasonal fluctuations and make their business decisions based on annual trends and not only the good times. A good operator will develop marketing tactics to attract customers during 'shoulder' and 'off season' periods such as special offers (eg. stay two nights, get one free etc.) to attract business.

Selling the Experience

Tourism is about creating and selling experiences. These are mostly 'intangible', or difficult to capture in words, making it difficult for operators to promote their product as customers can't generally sample or see the product before they buy. Brochures are widely used as one way to visually represent a tourism product to customers. Websites are also popular and can be a very effective method of promoting a tourism business to a global market. Whatever method is used, aim to help potential customers visualise and understand the experience that you are offering.

Agent's Commission

Commission is a recognised industry practice and is usually the major source of revenue for retail travel agents, inbound operators and wholesalers. Tourism operators need to understand how commissions are divided between the different levels of sellers and allow for the payment of commission in their prices.

Tourism Industry Structure

There is a number of government, government funded and industry bodies involved in tourism.

Department of Industry, Tourism and Resources

The department of industry, tourism and resources through its tourism division aims to develop, implement and deliver policies and programs which:

- encourage the development of tourism, sport and recreation
- identify opportunities in tourism, sport and recreation
- reduce barriers to industry development

— provide information to the tourism, sport and recreation industries to assist in decision making.

The focus of the department is largely in the policy area, and it is not generally involved in marketing activities.

The Marketing Process

Research shows that businesses that have a business plan have a greater chance of staying in business than those without a plan. Developing a marketing plan goes hand in hand with developing a business plan, but it is possible to develop a marketing plan as a stand alone document.

Many people often think that marketing is selling. Although selling is one function of marketing, there are many other aspects that need to be considered. One definition of marketing is:

> 'Marketing means selling your products and services at the right price, with the right promotion, to the right people, at the right location.... at a profit'.

A breakdown of the major components of marketing is as follows:

— Knowing who your customers are and what they want

— Developing products that meets their needs at a price that they are prepared to pay, and

— Promoting the product by a variety of means so that a purchase can occur.

In general, marketing activities fall into two general categories:

— *Researching your market* - discovering who your potential customers or markets are, and determining what they want, and

— *Reaching your market* - developing a program of activities that puts your product in the market place and making sure that customers know about it.

The Marketing Plan

These are the steps that need to be undertaken to develop a marketing plan:

1. *Business background*: What is your business about? What is your business mission, your goals and competitive advantage?
2. *Situations Analyses:* What are the internal and external factors that will impact on your business eg. industry trends, competitors, the economy, your financial resources, etc.
3. *Target Markets:* Who do you want to sell your product to and what are their needs?
4. *Marketing Mix:* Putting it all together - the 'Ps' of marketing
   - — Product or Service
   - — Packaging
   - — Place (or Distribution)
   - — Price
   - — Promotion
     - — Advertising
     - — Brochures
     - — Direct Marketing
     - — Trade Shows
     - — Consumer Promotions
     - — Publicity
     - — Personal Selling

- — Websites/Internet Marketing
- — Online Technologies

5. *Action Plan:* A summary of marketing initiatives that identifies who will be responsible for each initiative, how much they will cost and timeframes.
6. *Evaluation*: Evaluating the impact of marketing activities and modifying as required.

Business Background

Business mission

The Business Mission is a simple statement that describes what a business does or will do. This will also help to describe your business concept to others. The Business Mission can change as circumstances change - be prepared to review and modify if necessary.

Business goals

It is important to identify achievable objectives or goals for a business. These help to provide direction for decision making, measure the success of a business and provide a focus for staff.

Objectives are more helpful when they are quantified ie. include figures or other measures. Some examples of business objectives could be to:

- — increase the net return from the business from 10 per cent to 15 per cent; or
- — increase the average number of passengers on each tour from 12 to 15; or
- — increase room occupancy from 50 per cent to 60 per cent; or to
- — increase business by 20 per cent during shoulder periods.

Goals will be more valuable if they relate to a specific time-frame eg. 'to increase the average annual occupancy rate from 45 to 55 per cent within two years'. You may wish to add personal objectives for your business. These could relate to your financial security, how much time you wish to spend with your family, paying off your house mortgage etc.

Competitive advantage

A competitive advantage is the 'point of difference' that sets a business apart from its competitors.

Every business needs a competitive advantage. It gives you an edge over your competitors and provides a focus for marketing activities. One way of determining your point of difference is to examine your competitors in areas such as quality of products and services, location, price, etc. If you are unable to determine a competitive advantage by looking at your competitors, you may need to develop a feature that will give your business its marketing edge.

Examples of competitive advantages include:

— offering a unique product
— developing a product for a niche market
— offering superior facilities and/or services
— offering a more efficient service than your competitors
— offering a price advantage

In determining your competitive advantage, you must remember that it needs to be perceived by your customers as a benefit - something that will entice them to use your product as opposed to another operator.

Situation Analysis

Businesses don't operate in isolation. There are factors both within the control and beyond the control of businesses that can affect its success. These include the state of the economy, the general state of the tourism industry, the value of the currency, international events, what competitors are doing, etc. A full analysis of your business needs to consider the internal and external factors in terms of strengths, weaknesses, opportunities and threats. This review, known as a SWOT (Strengths, Weaknesses, Opportunities and Threats), will provide an overview of areas in need of attention and highlight opportunities that can be developed to expand the business.

External factors

External factors are factors beyond your control that could affect the business eg. the economy, technology, trends affecting the tourism industry, legal and political issues, competition, the environment etc.

These factors can have a major impact. For example, when the economy is in recession, or when interest rates and unemployment levels are high, people have less money and less demand for goods and services such as tours, accommodation etc. External factors are generally beyond the control of a business. But by being aware of these factors it's possible to make decisions that minimise possible negative impacts and maximise opportunities that may arise. For example, the current interest and publicity surrounding nature based tourism presents an opportunity for tour operators that can develop products to suit this market.

Internal factors

Internal factors are those over which you have some control, eg. equipment, financial resources, staff, etc.

Depending on the nature of your business, there will be a number of areas that need to be considered, for example, your physical resources - buildings and equipment. Are they being fully utilised? Can they cope with expansion? Then there are the financial resources of the business. Is your cash flow sufficient? Do you have access to additional funds to finance any growth activities? Is a lack of finance impeding your growth? Finally, you need to look at the experience and expertise of your staff. Are they motivated? Are they being used to the best of their ability? Is there any training available that could improve the efficiency and service offered by your business? The answers to these questions will assist you to understand what your business is able to achieve.

SWOT

A common way of summarising strengths, weaknesses, opportunities and threats is in a table format.

Strengths	*Weakness*
Opportunities	*Threats*

Use the table to:

— Build on your business strengths whenever possible. They should be exploited and reinforced to give your business an edge over competitors.

— Only correct weaknesses that are holding the business back - don't address minor areas which have little impact on the business.

— Maximise your business success by taking advantage of opportunities.

Competitor analysis

It is unlikely that you will operate a business that does not have competition. It is important that you identify who your competitors are, what their strengths and weaknesses are, how much of the business or market share they have and how much of the market share you have or want to have.

We have already referred to the need to consider your competitors to determine your competitive advantage. You can also use a competitor analysis to maintain your advantage and seize opportunities that may arise from the actions of your competitors.

Target Market

Successful marketing is based on understanding who you wish to sell or market your product to. You can help to determine your market and understand more about their characteristics by undertaking market research.

There are various ways of identifying different customer groups, or target markets.

These include:

— *Demographics* - age, gender, income, family size, and structure, education, occupation etc.

— *Origin* - where they live

— *Socio-economic class* - professional, non-professional

— *Lifestyle* - 'pleasure seeker', 'achiever', etc

Put another way, you need to ask yourself questions about who your likely customers will be:

— What age groups best describes your market?

— Is your product aimed at males, females, or both?

— Will it suit singles, couples, or families?

— Is your product aimed at a specific group of people and if so what group? eg. bird-watchers, tennis players, etc.

By identifying your target market/s you will be able to develop a customer profile - which will tell you how your target market thinks and behaves - what newspapers/ magazines they are likely to read, when are they likely to travel, etc. This information will be useful in developing promotional strategies to reach potential customers.

Marketing Mix

The marketing mix is 'the way that you put together the factors under your control to satisfy the needs of your customers. These are often known as the 'P's' of marketing - Product, Packaging, Placing Yourself in the Marketplace - (or Distribution), Promotion and Price.

Product or service

This refers to the product or service that you sell eg. tours, accommodation, souvenirs, meals, etc. Your product needs to reflect your research of who your customers are and what they want.

There are many factors that affect the way that you develop your product or service. You first need to identify exactly what your product is - what it includes and where the value is in what you are offering. Whilst this may appear obvious, there are many failed businesses that did not fully understand what their product was. As part of identifying your product, you need to consider where it fits in the market place ie. its position in relation to other operators. For instance, some accommodation operators position their property at the top end of the market, while others will develop their product to meet the needs of budget travellers. You also need to develop an image that is appropriate for your product and its position in the market. Your image will be communicated through your business name, brochures, letterhead, business cards, signage, and advertising. It will also be represented by the appearance of your premises and staff.

Associated with image is branding, which makes your product or service distinctive by the use of slogans, logos, distinctive colours and graphics. Well chosen brand names and logos can add value to a product or service and can be used with great effect to gain customer loyalty.

Product life cycle

Each product or service that enters the marketplace has a distinct life cycle. This is not difficult to understand when you consider how often fashion tastes change and how cuisines that are in vogue one year, are unheard of the next. The same occurs with holiday destinations and tourism products.

There are four stages to the product life cycle:

1. *Introduction:* The product is introduced into the market. Sales are slow as the product becomes known. Nil or very low profit is experienced due to the expense of developing and introducing the product.
2. *Growth:* A period when the product is accepted by the market place which results in growing sales and profit.
3. *Maturity:* Sales slow as the product achieves acceptance by the majority of potential buyers. Profits stabilise or decline. Increased marketing is required to attract sales.
4. *Decline:* Sales show a strong decline and profits drop.

By considering the above cycle you can plan changes to existing products or introduce new products as they reach the maturity stage to maintain business growth.

Packaging

Packaging is the way that associated products and services are put together to form a package deal. A motel operator may develop a package that includes transport, tickets to a local concert and evening meal as part of a total package. The operator benefits by ensuring that guests dine in-house, while customers don't have to spend time considering their options.

Packaging offers great opportunities to target specific markets and explore new ones, particularly during shoulder and off season periods when business is slow eg. 'book five nights, get two free, plus a fruit basket and chocolates on arrival!'. Operators in regional areas can work together to develop attractive deals that will encourage visits to their region. Not only does each individual operator benefit by such arrangements, but the region in general benefits by greater visitor numbers and increased expenditure.

Place (Distribution)

Once you have a clear understanding of what your product is, you need to make it accessible to the public. It is likely that you will be targeting your product to markets interstate or overseas. To reach these markets you may use the services of agents, or intermediaries to act on your behalf and take bookings. Intermediaries include travel agents, travel wholesalers and inbound tour operators. Using intermediaries is the most common way of broadening the distribution base of your product and are usually necessary if a business is to expand.

There are four main channels of distribution:

— *Direct to the customer (no commission payable):* Where the customer books directly with you as a result of seeing your brochure, advertising, website or is referred to you by a personal recommendation.

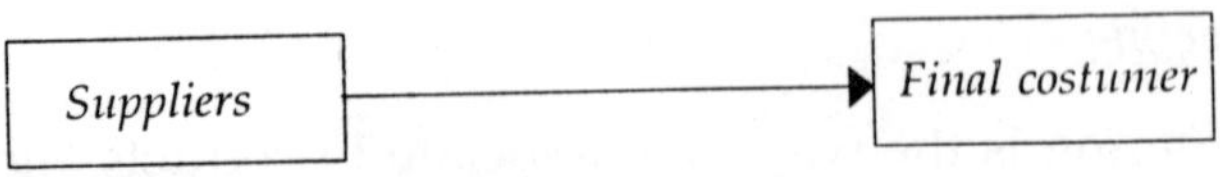

— *Via a retailer (normally 10% commission payable)*: Where the customer books your product at a retail travel agency

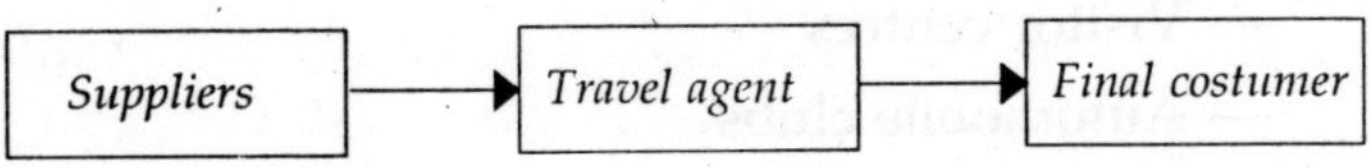

— *Via a wholesaler and a retailer (normally 20%-25% commission payable)*: Where the customer books your product from a brochure that has been put together by a tour wholesaler and sold through a retail travel agency

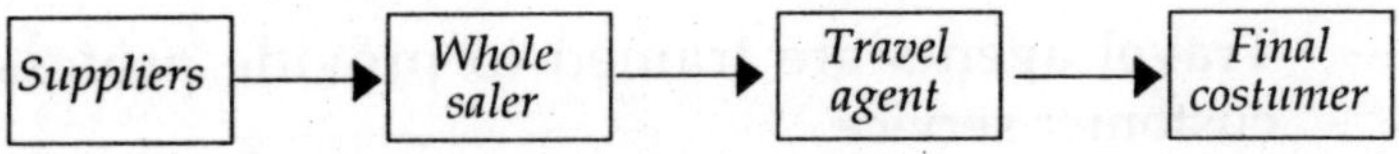

— *Via an inbound tour operator, wholesaler and retailer (normally up to 30% commission payable):* Where your product is packaged by an inbound tour operator that is included in an international wholesale holiday brochure and sold via an overseas retail travel agency To understand these distribution channels, each of the intermediaries is considered in greater detail below:

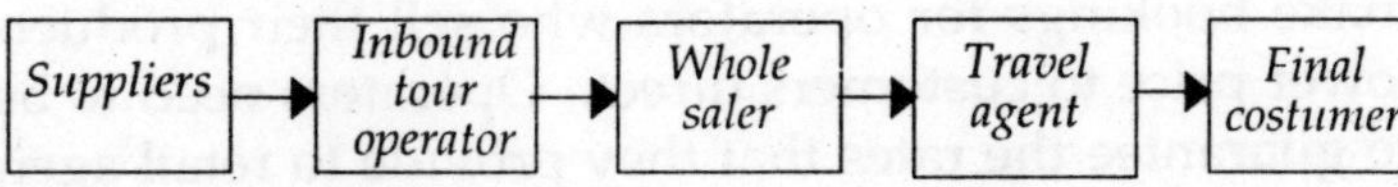

Retail travel agents

Retail travel agents sell travel services direct to customers and act on their behalf to book and purchase holiday packages, travel, accommodation, tours and so on. In addition to providing a booking service, retail agents have an important role in providing information. Examples of key retailers include:

— Independent travel agents, or group travel agency networks.

— Government tourist centres

— Visitor centres

— Automobile clubs

Retail travel agents provide advantages for both customers and tourism operators:

— They are a one-stop travel shop - agents can assist customers with several travel queries and make all bookings at the one location

— Single charge billing - customers only pay one account to the travel agent

— Travel agents are trained to provide professional customer service

— Holidays are pre-paid and pre-ticketed prior to travel, giving the customer peace of mind

Rates and commissions

Travel agents are generally paid 10 per cent of the retail price as a booking fee, although this rate does vary and can be as high as 20 per cent. It is most important that agents and operators charge the same price. Travel agents will not make bookings for operators who sell their products at a lower price to customers direct. Operators need to be able to guarantee the rates that they provide to retail agents.

It is the responsibility of tourism operators to ensure that travel agents are familiar with their products. Retail agents are able to book many destinations and products making it difficult for them to be up to date with every tour product. Operators can use some of the following ways to keep travel agents informed:

— Make sales calls.

— Provide special rates to people working in retail agencies to encourage staff to experience their product

— Offer agents a familiarisation of your tour/service

— Send regular newsletters or other direct forms of communications (e-mail, fax)

— Ensure that agents have current brochures and rates

— Participate in wholesale programs

Above all, tourism operators must be able to respond to travel agent enquiries and bookings promptly. Not all retail travel agents book individual tourism operators. Many agents specialise in international holidays or only book fully inclusive packaged holidays, which offer high commission payments. Other agents, particularly those in large networks, have a 'preferred' range of products that they sell and operators may need to offer heavily discounted rates to be included in this list.

Wholesalers

Wholesalers package tour programs including travel, accommodation, and tours that are sold to the public via retail travel agents. Wholesalers do not sell directly to customers. Wholesalers link individual tourism operators with retailers. They consider what type of tour program would appeal to a particular market and package the program accordingly. Wholesale packages are usually priced lower than if the consumer was to book each component direct. Wholesalers are able to achieve this price advantage because of the volume of business and exposure they generate.

Benefits to Operators of being included in a Wholesale Program:

— A brochure is produced and distributed to travel agents.

— An industry launch is usually held to promote the program.

— The wholesaler's representatives will conduct sales calls on retail travel agents to promote the program and operators in it.

— Wholesalers have computerised reservation systems to record bookings. Many of these are global systems allowing travel agents worldwide to book products in the program.

— Familiarisation visits for the retail industry are conducted to give front-line sales staff an opportunity to experience the product first hand.

— Familiarisation visits by the media are conducted to generate publicity for the program.

— Wholesalers generally undertake advertising campaigns aimed at both consumers and retail travel agents.

Customers benefit by the ease of booking through a retail agent and the knowledge that the tourism products are of good quality - wholesalers will rarely include a product in their brochures that don't have a proven track record.

Every wholesaler will have a different cost structure for operators to participate in their programs. In most cases, wholesalers aim to produce a brochure that is funded by participating operators, ie. operators pay for space in the brochure. While this rate will vary, it is generally reasonable in comparison to the cost that operators would have to pay to produce and distribute their own brochure. Wholesalers are an important intermediary and have the potential to provide 'top up' business.

Paying commission

Paying commission is a way of life in the tourism industry and it is a concept that tourism operators need to understand to take advantage of the distribution channels available.

There are two ways of reaching potential clients:

— *Directly* - advertising, brochure distribution, website

— *Indirectly* - using retail travel agents, wholesalers and inbound tour operators There is a cost attached to both methods that needs to be considered in your financial feasibility assessment and the cost of tourism products.

Tourism operators do find difficulty in justifying the commission required by some agents, yet the costs in accessing these markets are generally way beyond the reach of small operators and the cost of paying commission is often balanced out by the number of bookings received direct by the business, which don't incur a commission. It is important that you keep a record of all sales and identify the source of all bookings - direct, travel agent, wholesaler etc. as this breakdown could influence the future selling price of your product.

Inbound tour operators

Inbound tour operators act on behalf of national and international tour wholesalers to organise the 'land/ground' content of a tour programme. Inbound tour operators act as intermediaries between wholesalers and tourism operators. They are usually able to negotiate better rates due to the volume and regular use of the tourism products they book.

Inbound tour operators put together different tourism products to create packages to suit the needs of different inbound markets. These include:

— *The individual traveller*, known as the 'fully independent traveller' or FIT. This market buys from a wholesaler's brochure or buys a specially tailored itinerary.

— *The group traveller*, known as the 'group inclusive tour' or GIT. They can also buy from a wholesaler's brochure or have a specially tailored itinerary created to suit their needs.

— *Incentive traveller*. Many businesses reward performance by providing travel rewards to employees as incentives. These travel arrangements usually require a tailor made product that is at the top-end of the market.

— *Convention traveller.* Conventions involve the movement of large numbers of people and inbound operators can develop pre- and post-convention tours.

Inbound tour operators conduct a number of activities to attract the interest of overseas wholesalers and retail agents and to make them aware of the services and products.

The benefits of working with an inbound tour operator include:

— They create individually tailored packages eg. farm-stay, self-drive, nature-based tourism, special events, etc

— They attend trade workshops, missions and shows

— They provide international exposure for your product

Inbound tour operators will require a net rate from the tourism operator that is usually 30 per cent, but could be up to 40 per cent off the normal selling rate. As for wholesalers, rates will need to be valid for a twelve month period. This commission is divided between travel agent (usually 10 per cent), the overseas wholesaler (10 per cent but can be up to 15 per cent), and the inbound operator (10 per cent but may be up to 15 per cent).

Coach tour operators

Operators of tourist attractions or accommodation establishments may also wish to consider attracting business from coach tour operators. Attracting the interest of a coach operator may take time. Each year coach companies receive hundreds of requests from tourist attractions and other businesses to be included in their itineraries.

Send coach operators an introductory letter, brochure and invitation to visit your business or perhaps offer to host a lunch or overnight stay, if relevant. After these initial approaches, maintain regular contact.

How to encourage coach tour operators to use your product and build relationships:

— Provide a quality product and demonstrate a commitment to customer service
— Ensure that your offer suits the requirements of the coach tour operator
— Make it easy for drivers to drop off passengers, manoeuvre coaches, and park
— Make drivers feel welcome
— Adhere to negotiated rates. Don't try to suddenly increase your charges
— Stick to agreed times - coach tours operate to strict timetables and will be inconvenienced by any unscheduled changes
— Don't complain if passenger numbers are initially lower than expected. It often takes time to build up business.

When you commit to an inbound tour operator, wholesaler, or coach tour operator, you must guarantee your service, irrespective of passenger numbers. Inbound tour operators and wholesalers will refuse to make reservations for operators that have minimum number restrictions or are prone to cancelling tours. Similarly, coach tour operators will not visit attractions, or use accommodation, which don't provide quality service every visit.

Inbound tour operators, wholesalers, and coach operators don't usually include tour products in their programs that don't have a proven track record. It may be necessary for you to be in business for more than two years before these operators will consider using your product.

These operators also plan and book their programs up to two years in advance. Be patient and cultivate relationships so that when an opportunity does arise your business will be 'top of mind'.

Price

The issue of setting rates is a complex one, and needs to be part of a detailed and objective financial feasibility for your business. In the context of marketing, varying the cost of your product can be used as a sales promotion tool. You can consider various sales tools such as discounting, cash back vouchers and give-aways.

Often, reducing the price is seen as the only way to beat the competition, but beware - reducing your price could reduce your profit. You need to consider how discounting will affect the willingness of consumers to purchase your product and how great the effect will be. In developing a price strategy you need to look at what your competitors are charging. Before entering into a price war you need to consider whether this will affect the perception of your product by consumers. It is possible that products offered at lower prices will be perceived as having less value.

An option to price discounting is to 'value add'. This can be achieved by offering extra services which will be perceived by the consumer as a bonus, but which do not add a major cost to you.

Promotion

So far, we have been considering the 'behind the scenes' elements of the marketing process. The next stage in the marketing process is to promote your product to potential customers and generate sales. There are many useful promotional tools available. Unfortunately, many operators are tempted to try too many of these at the one time.

In determining the most effective way of communicating your message to your target market, consider your customer profile - what do your potential customers read? Where do they go? Who influences them? etc. For example there would be little value in advertising a backpacker hostel in a business magazine, and similarly little would be gained from advertising a five star hotel in a magazine aimed at teenagers. Knowing who your potential customers are will help you chose the most effective promotion tools.

Some of the proven promotion options include:

— Advertising
— Brochures
— Direct Marketing
— Trade Shows
— Consumer Promotions
— Public Relations
— Personal Selling
— Online Technologies

Advertising

Advertising includes mass media such as newspapers, magazines, radio, television and billboards. It can reach many people at once and the same message can be repeated many times. There are advantages and disadvantages to advertising. It can be very expressive and emotional in its appeal and can reach a large audience. On the other hand, it is expensive and impersonal - it is one way communication. There are many opportunities for cooperative advertising where several businesses or organisations work together to produce and pay for a joint advertisement. It is sometimes possible to arrange editorial in publications in which you advertise. This is when the newspaper, magazine or other mediums produces a feature article about your business (often on the basis of information you provide) that supports your ad. This is often call 'advertorial' and can be effective as it appears to be more objective and have more credibility than advertising.

One form of advertising that can be cost-effective for tourism operators is newspaper advertising.

There are two main types of newspaper ads:

— Display ads - these can appear in the travel pages or in the general news section of a newspaper.

— Lineage ads - 'line ads' are so-called because you are charged on a per line basis. Line ads may be. placed in the classified section or a special classified section in the travel pages.

Display ads are much more expensive than line ads, however, this means of advertising is often an important source of business for small operators.

Publications

There is a range of publications that offer advertising space for tourism operators, including local tourist guides produced by visitor centres and commercial publications. It is likely that you will be inundated with offers and requests for advertising. Ask what the print run is, where the publications will be distributed and who they are aimed at when considering the potential benefit to your business.

Brochures

Brochures are an important means of conveying your image and message to potential customers. Brochures should do more than describe the how, what, where and when of your business; they need to be visually appealing and convey the right amount of information to stimulate interest and demand.

Brochures need to be easy to read with an eye-catching heading, a simple message, and easy-to-read print. They should be attractive and present the right image for the type of experience you are offering eg. using an earthy coloured recycled paper would suit a nature-based tour, whereas a glossy, four colour brochure may be more appropriate for an up-market hotel. It is important to also remember to allow plenty of 'white space' (blank areas) as cluttered brochures look busy and may turn people off from reading them.

There are some basic decisions that need to be made early in the brochure production process. eg:

— What do you want your brochure to do?

— Who is the brochure aimed at?

— What size/style should it be?

— What is your budget?

— How many do I need?

Your brochure should be consistent with other brochures in the industry. These are usually either A4 in size (210mm x 297mm) or DL (210mm x 100mm). Both these sizes fit standard size envelopes.

Colour can be used to make your brochure "stand out" but be careful not to use colours which are too bright and which do not suit the experience you are selling.

What to Include in a Brochure : Some Tips Be sure that you include:

— Tour details - the number of days, departure dates, the itinerary, departure or pick-up points, start and finish times

— Booking conditions

— Contact details for bookings (phone/fax numbers, email and web addresses)

— Validity dates of the brochure

- — Tariffs or tours prices - this section should include discounts for pensioners, students, etc. and list what is and is not included in the price
- — Alternative booking agencies
- — Room on the back of the brochure for a travel agents stamp
- — Transport division, department for planning and infrastructure, licence number, if relevant

A map is useful, particularly if you are intending to promote your product overseas or interstate. Maps should show the location of your product.

When drafting the copy (or words) of your brochure make sure you do not include any unacceptable (illegal) clauses or misleading information. There has been an increase in the number of legal actions bought against operators for loss of enjoyment or deceptive and misleading advertising. It is essential to honestly represent your product/service in promotional material. If in doubt, seek legal advice.

Once you have worked out the details, there are a number of product factors that need to be considered:

- — Design and artwork - how will it look?
- — The words, or copy - write the information in a way that is catchy and to the point. Be sure to check grammar and spelling.
- — Photographs - these need to be of good quality and present an accurate representation of the experience.
- — Negative preparation - needed when you print a colour brochure
- — Printing - you need to decide what paper stock to use and how many brochures you want printed.

You may have the skills or be willing to tackle part of producing the brochure yourself. If not, there is a host of designers, photographers, freelance writers and printers that can assist. If you are in doubt, it may be wise to seek expert advice, as errors may be costly to correct. Make sure you also proof read your brochure carefully before it goes to print.

The impact of your brochure will be dependent on effective distribution. You must consider who you want to distribute your brochure to and have a system in place to update stocks as required.

Travel agents with a propensity to sell your product Brochure distribution companies specialise in distributing brochures to the tourism industry. For a fee, these companies store brochures, control brochure flow/stock usage, provide monthly stock movement reports, and undertake bulk mail-outs. Travel agents/visitor centres order brochure supplies directly from the brochure distribution company, relieving you of the time consuming task of canvassing all your agents to ascertain their stock levels.

Direct marketing

Direct marketing means contacting - by mail, telephone, fax or email - potential customers. It also includes coupon advertising where potential customers send in a coupon asking for more information.

Direct marketing usually involves sending messages (brochures, letters) to a database, which is simply a list of potential customers that have been collected because of common characteristic eg. occupation, income level, postcode or by business type or interest such as travel agents, inbound tour operators, bowling clubs, ornithological associations etc. Databases are available in different formats including mailing labels, computer disks, and lists. They are available from a variety of sources including firms that specialise in compiling databases.

An advantage of direct marketing is that it is more personal, however, it does not have the same penetration as general advertising. The success of any direct marketing activity will be determined by the quality of the database and the quality and impact of the message or offer.

Trade shows

Trade shows provide the opportunity for tourism operators/RTOs to promote their business/region to the travel industry. Exhibitors, called 'sellers', usually book a space or booth. Appointments are made with 'buyers', who, depending on the type of trade show, could be retail travel agents, inbound tour operators and/or tour wholesalers. Appointments are usually 10 to 20 minutes long, during which sellers give a presentation on their product.

Trade shows are a cost-effective means of servicing a large number of agents in a short period of time. It is possible to share a booth at some shows with another operator, preferably one that is not in direct competition to your business, to reduce costs. The success of your participation will depend on having effective, good quality promotional materials and a package and/or product that buyers can sell. It may take up to two years to gain results from participating in a trade show as wholesalers usually prepare their packages two years in advance.

To maximise the value of participating in trade shows, it is important to follow up with buyers after the show either by letter or email. Your hard work and investment can be wasted if you do not maintain contact with, and the interest of, buyers. Trade show organisers generally set selection criteria for each show to ensure that a high standard of tourism product is presented. Most shows are organised well in advance and participants are generally required to book at least six months in advance.

Consumer promotions

Consumer promotions or shows provide tourism operators with the opportunity to promote direct to consumers - ie. the general public. Consumer promotions can vary greatly and target different market segments. They can include caravan and camping shows and holiday and travel shows.

Space is allocated to tourism operators and RTOs to promote their products. Booth costs are determined by size and/or location. Many shows are held on the weekend, however, some shows run up to seven days.

Consumer shows provide operators with the opportunity to talk personally with potential customers, conduct market research by talking to the public and to network with other operators.

You will generally have the opportunity of selecting a site from a floor plan of the exhibition area. Good site selection will help to ensure the success of your participation. Good sites include corner locations on main aisles; main aisles as opposed to secondary aisles; sites leading to/from restaurants, toilets and entrances; and in the instance of multi-hall venues, sites in the main hall. These locations will generally attract greater traffic flows than other areas.

When participating in consumer promotions you are competing with many other tourism operators and destinations. To maximise your involvement, make sure that your stand is attractive and eye-catching and that you have plenty of brochures available for distribution. Consider having a competition relating to your product or other 'catches' such as giveaways to attract attention.

Public relations

Tour operators can draw attention to their business by being 'newsworthy' and gaining free publicity in newspapers and magazines. Large businesses may employ a public relations (PR) professional to generate news stories and media releases which are distributed to the media.

While smaller operators may not be able to employ the services of a PR professional, you can derive great benefits by maintaining a close liaison with your local media and travel writers of State newspapers. Keep them informed of new developments that might be of interest and have a go at writing your own media release.

Some tips for writing a media release are given blow:

— Media releases need to be to the point - try and keep them to one A4 page, double spaced.·

— Your release should include the Who, Where, What, When, Why, and How of your story.

— The first paragraph introduces the story and should attract the editor's attention ie. it contains your main message, or 'news'.

— The following paragraphs need to provide further detail to support your 'news'.They should include details, in descending order of importance, because editors are likely to shorten stories from the bottom up.

Be sure to:

— Be specific, don't overuse superlatives, eg. the 'most magnificent', the 'biggest and best' etc.

— Make sure names are spelt correctly

— Keen the language simple, don't use jargon

— Include quotes from relevant people - this gives the story credibility

— Always include the date and a contact phone number for further information

— If your story is more than one page, include page numbers

— There are many state and national magazines and journals in circulation, and their editors are always on the look out for interesting stories.

Media familiarisations

Familiarisations, or 'famils' are media visits that are organised by the state tourism commission or department. These visits generate significant publicity for the host conutry and its tourism products included in the famils. Visits are organised for national and international media in accordance with marketing objectives and strategies of tourism commission or department. Media are invited to visit the state and to write or broadcast their experiences on return to their point of origin. Tourism operators that participate in famils need to observe some general guidelines that will maximise the benefits from their involvement and contribute to the success of the visit. Where there are a similar range of products, preference is generally given to tourism network members and accredited operators.

Radio and television

There are opportunities to promote your tourism product using television and radio. These include interviews, donating prizes for competitions, or using community service announcements to promote an achievement or activity of your business (this is more achievable in regional areas). Holiday and lifestyle programs also offer excellent promotional opportunities.

Personal selling

An important way of selling your product is by personal sales calls, generally to retail travel agents, but also to inbound and coach operators and tour wholesalers, depending on what is appropriate for your business.

Sales staff may also represent your business at trade and consumer shows, and participate in promotion activities. Many small operators are not able to employ sales staff or sufficient sales staff to service all markets eg. the eastern states and overseas and may engage the services of a sales representation company to cover specific markets.

There are benefits to using a representative to act on your behalf:

— They provide a sales office or point of contact for agents. This can be particularly useful if, for example, you run a tour yourself and can't be contacted easily.

— They often provide a broad range of services and can assist with such things as advertising, direct mail and brochure production.

— They provide a direct liaison with agents and can help you to focus on the more productive ones.

Sales representation has a cost. It may be more economical to employ your own staff than using a sales representative to act on your behalf. Above all else, don't expect overnight miracles and treat your sales representative as part of the team.

Online Technologies

Websites: Advances in communications have generated a host of new ways of marketing any business. Effective websites need to offer current, interesting information based on researching consumer needs. Sites should showcase your products and services, contact details and be interactive, ie. users can ask questions, give feedback or make bookings online. Websites can be a particularly effective promotional tool as they have the capacity to portray the experience of a tourism product that a brochure or advertisement can't. It is important that sites are enjoyable to visit and that they are updated regularly to attract repeat visitors. Consider adding a visitor's book, include copies of past newsletters and other items of interest such as newspaper articles or testimonials. Ensure that your web address is featured on all your marketing tools to encourage visits to the site. Other online advertising opportunities include banner advertising on other websites. You can also offer reciprocal online advertising by including links on your website to companies or sites that complement your business and have other sites include links to yours.

Email: Email provides a cost effective way of distributing newsletters and other messages such as special offers. Be sure to obtain email addresses from clients or potential clients. These can be very useful databases.

Action Plan

You are now ready to put all your marketing decisions into an action plan, which is a summary of all marketing initiatives that have been developed after considering each of the different elements of marketing. Your action plan is best presented in a simple table format that clearly identifies:

— Name of the marketing action/project
— Who will be responsible for carrying out the action/project
— What resources are required eg. cost, equipment, staff resources, etc.
— Timeframe
— Who will monitor the activity to ensure that it has been undertaken successfully

The action plan is a summary of the 'doing part' of the marketing plan and will be the most referred to section of the plan. Distribute copies of the action plan to staff - this will help everyone to know where the business is heading and what marketing activities are underway and planned for the future.

Action plans are usually produced for a one year period, although they can include strategies that are being developed over several years. It is important that action plans are regularly reviewed and updated as required. Plans need to be flexible so that they can take advantage of opportunities as they arise or as circumstances change eg. new competitors, changing economic conditions. If the action plan isn't being implemented, or there are difficulties associated with achieving specific strategies, it may be necessary to make alterations to make them more realistic.It may be useful to prepare monthly reports as part of the monitoring process.

Budget

Your Marketing Plan will have a cost. There are two options - you identify the marketing activities that you would like to undertake if money were no object and then prioritise according to the resources available, or, establish the budget that you are prepared to allocate to marketing and then allocate costs against those activities that you determine to be necessary to the success of your business. It is important to include a contingency figure in your budget. It is not always possible to be aware of every marketing opportunity and worthwhile marketing opportunities can arise at short notice.

Monitoring and Evaluation

Marketing is an ongoing process. Plans need to be monitored and reviewed regularly. Evaluating your marketing plan will also help you to prepare more realistic and achievable plan in the future. Ways of measuring the performance of your marketing plan include changes to sales figures, market share, and profit. This will require keeping accurate figures to monitor where business is being generated and if it can be directly attributed to marketing initiatives.

Rules for Successful Tourism Marketing

Tourism is an important economic activity because it brings in dollars from outside the community. It continues to be a fast growing sector and is typically included among the top three industries in the country. In addition, tourism provides a "front-door" to non-tourism economic development efforts such as business recruitment. Following are some rules for successful tourism.

Success Begins With a Good Plan: Creating a Tourism Development & Marketing Plan is the first rule for successful tourism. The plan should include several details like product development, upgrades and improvements, repositioning and/or branding, attractions and events, visitor amenities and services, marketing and public relations, public/private partnerships, recruitment, funding and budgets, and organizational responsibilities. The plan should integrate existing comprehensive plans and economic development and Main Street efforts.

Importance of Front-line Sales: Your front-line employees can be your most valuable sales team. This is because they establish the first contact with the customer. The front-line employees should be knowledgeable about your community and should promote other stores, attractions and amenities to visitors to keep them in the area longer.

Critical Mass: In order to attract and keep visitors in your community, there must be several retail and dining establishments within walking distance. Shopping and dining in a pedestrian setting is one of the top activities for visitors. An average rule of thumb for rural communities is to have nine retail stores and four dining/treats establishments within two or three blocks.

Turn Negatives Into Positives: Almost every community and attraction has its challenges. Think creatively on how to convert these negatives into positives. You can then attract people to your area using clever promotional tactics. For example, when an article in the Washington Post labeled Battle Mountain, Nevada the "Armpit of America", the town took a positive spin on that title by having an annual event sponsored by Old Spice drawing thousands of visitors.

Be Unique: I n order to be successful, you must be worth the trip. A visitor must be able to differentiate you from the competition and you must strive to be creative and set yourself apart from others. Being unique will make a visitor travel the extra distance.

Telling Stories: Museums and interpretive centers should always tell stories, not just display artifacts. Stories can keep visitors in the area longer, which means additional spending. Visitors also remember stories, and captivating stories are told and passed on to others. More people pick destinations by word of mouth than any other method.

Four-Times Rule: People are willing to travel a distance if you offer something that appeals to them. There should be enough for visitors to see and do in your area. In general, you should be able to keep visitors busy four times longer than it took them to get there.

Marketing vs. Product Development: Before you market your community, make sure it is appealing to customers. If your product is not of great quality, then your marketing efforts are wasted. Product development should always be a top priority, and it never ends. Having a good mix of product development and marketing is also important.

Selling the Experience: Always sell the experience associated with an activity and not the place. If you are using pictures in your marketing campaign, avoid using scenic images. Scenery lasts in the mind for only a few moments. Instead, use images of people laughing and having fun. Viewers are more likely to remember images that include people's emotions.

Branding: Even at the community level, branding is critical for success in tourism. Branding is much more than just a logo; it is what sets you apart from your competition, it is your image and your value. Do not try to be "all things to all people."

WOW Photography: Nothing sells tourism like great photography. Photographs used for tourism purposes should have a "wow" appeal in the viewer and should make the viewer want to go to the place depicted. As mentioned earlier, you are trying to sell an experience and your photos should evoke emotion in the viewer. Photography should be the key element in brochures, public relation efforts, and especially on the web.

Close the Sale: Most communities and attractions spend a significant amount of money on advertising. The primary "call to action" in advertising is to get the potential customer to call and get a brochure, or for them to visit your web site. If this is the case, the brochure and web site should be good enough to close the sale. Otherwise, your advertising effort is largely wasted. Pay attention to certain small details while advertising. For example, for brochures, the best colors to use are red and yellow as these colors get the viewers attention. In addition, most brochures end up in racks along with scores of other brochures and the top three inches is all that is visible to the potential customer.

Public Relations: Even though you need both, publicity is much more important than advertising. Implementing a professional public relations campaign can have several benefits: it will build brand, improve your image, increase credibility and will provide a greater return on investment than advertising alone. Public relation is how you build your brand and advertising is how you maintain your position. Studies show that for every $1 invested into a public relations campaign, you get a $3 return.

Effective Web Sites: According to a Nielsen/Netratings study, nearly 75% of the U.S. population has access to the

Internet from home. In addition, 94% of Internet users make travel arrangements using the Web. The Internet is by far the number one resource for planning travel and vacations. If you have a tourism related web site, can your potential customers find you easily on the Web? How does your web site compare with the competition? Make the online experience interactive for the customer and remember to promote attractions, not just the place or your organization. Several thousands of dollars spent on web site development and maintenance is not a waste of money. You can even make sure your web site is displayed at the top of a Web search by paying a fee.

Frequency in Advertising: Frequency is more important than variety in placing advertising. People viewing your advertisement should develop Top of Mind Awareness (TOMA). For example, when the words "fast food" are mentioned, most people think of McDonalds because they make a good use of frequency in advertising.

4

Growth in Hospitality Service

The growth in the services sector of the worldwide economy has been phenomenal in the last 25 years. In the United States, services currently account for more than 75 percent of the gross domestic product (GDP), which is a popular measure of an economy's productivity. Similarly, on an international scale, services continue to account for an ever-increasing percentage of economic activity. Most new jobs are created in the service sector, and the growth in the hospitality and tourism industry is a major contributor.

Until the mid-1980s, the emphasis within the marketing community was on products. Now services have surpassed products and have taken on a more important role in marketing. Services, such as those offered by providers in the hospitality and tourism industry, have developed marketing strategies and practices that are unique. It has been established that the strategies, tactics, and practices that have been used successfully for product marketers do not always work successfully for those who market services. With the distinct differences between products and services in mind, the field of services marketing has evolved.

Unlike products, which are tangible, services are usually intangible. A service is not a physical good; rather, it is the performance of an act or a deed. This performance often requires consumers to be present during the production or delivery of the service. Service industries, including hospitality and tourism, are actually selling consumers an experience. Services have been defined to "include all economic activities whose output is not a physical product or construction, is generally consumed at the time it is produced, and provides added value in forms that are essentially intangible concerns of its first purchaser."Service employees such as front desk agents, housekeepers, hostesses, wait staff, car rental agents, flight attendants, and travel agents are responsible for creating positive experiences for customers. These frontline employees are critical to the success of service firms and play boundary-spanning roles because of their direct contact with customers. These roles are important because customers' perceptions of service firms are formed as a result of their dealings with the boundary-spanning employees.

Several reasons underlie the remarkable growth in services. Two leading services marketing experts, Christopher Lovelock and Lauren Wright, cite numerous reasons for this growth:

Changing patterns of government regulation: The reduction in government regulation has spurred the growth of services. In recent years, there has been a very noticeable shift toward the government taking a much less active role in the regulation of business activities. The most noteworthy of these shifts have been in the airline, trucking, telecommunication, and electrical generation and distribution industries. All of these industries have seen significant changes, as the barriers to entry have been removed and regulations governing such marketing elements as price have also been relaxed or entirely removed.

Relaxation of professional association restrictions on marketing: A new element of competition has been introduced into professions such as law and medicine as more of the practitioners in these areas advertise their services. Bans or restrictions on promotion have been largely removed. Within the hospitality and tourism industry, standards have also changed. We have seen an increase in advertising focusing on direct comparisons, or attacks, on competitors' products and services. This type of advertising strategy creates, or sustains, the perception of superiority in the mind of the consumer in favor of the brand being advertised.

Privatization of some public and nonprofit services: The term privatization was first used in Great Britain when the government adopted the policy of returning national industries from government to private ownership. This transformation has resulted in a greater emphasis on cost containment and a clearer focus on customers' needs. Later, in Central and Eastern Europe, following the fall of communism, we witnessed a continuing transformation from planned or government-run economies to market-driven economies fueled by private companies. Many of these countries' governments have released the control of airlines and travel agencies to private firms.

Technological innovation: Technology continues to alter the way firms do business and interact with consumers. In all types of businesses, consumers take a more active role in the service delivery process. For example, airlines, in an effort to reduce labor costs and increase speed of service to customers, have aggressively promoted self-check-in, both at the ticket counter and through their Web sites prior to arrival at the airport. Customers print boarding passes, receipts, and other documents without intervention by an airline employee. Express checkout for hotel guests has been in place for many years, but hotel chains continue to experiment with ways to enhance the service, thereby reducing labor costs and/or increasing the customers' perceived value.

In other settings, touch-screen computers collect feedback from guests, in much the same manner that comment cards have been used previously. The ease with which a company can maintain and access a database has permitted the development of sophisticated reservation systems and has led to more sophisticated frequent traveler programs. The use of more sophisticated reservations and property management systems has allowed hospitality and tourism firms to improve the level of service provided to guests. Guest history data serve as another example of how a hospitality organization can use technology to gain a competitive advantage. If a hotel guest requests a specific type of pillow, staff can record this preference within the individual's guest history file. When this guest checks into another hotel operated by the chain, the items that were previously requested can be waiting, without the guest even having to request them.

Growth in service chains and franchise networks: Much of the growth in service firms, including the hospitality industry, has been the direct result of franchising efforts by some of the major companies. Franchising represents a contractual arrangement whereby one firm (the franchisor) licenses a number of other firms (the franchisees) to use the franchisor's name and business practices. Notable lodging organizations such as Choice Hotels International and Marriott International, as well as food service firms such as McDonald's, Burger King, Taco Bell, and Wendy's, have all used franchising as a major vehicle for growth. The continued growth of the hospitality industry by means of franchising has put additional stress on independent owners and operators. In fact, each year the percentage of hospitality and tourism operations that are independently operated decreases.

Internationalization and globalization: Increasing shareholder value often remains directly associated with increasing company sales and profits, and globalization is one means of achieving this. As more and more of the prime locations are developed domestically, companies look internationally for expansion opportunities. This has been particularly true for fast-food franchisors: a significant proportion of their expansion during the last few years has occurred outside of their traditional domestic markets.

Pressures to improve productivity: In many industries within the service economy, competition stays very intense. This factor, when combined with the pressure from investors for higher returns on capital, has resulted in pressure to increase productivity and reduce costs. In many cases, managers seek to reduce labor costs by running leaner operations or using technology to replace humans for some tasks An example of this was when Delta Airlines encouraged passengers to check in via the Internet, thereby reducing the number of passengers who wanted to check in at the airport. They offered an incentive of 1,000 extra frequent-flyer miles to any passenger who used this service. While increasing productivity and profits remains a highly desirable goal, it must not be done at the expense of longterm customer satisfaction. Without long-term satisfaction, future profitability may exist in jeopardy.

The service quality movement: With the advent of consumerism, the public's perception is that service quality has declined. In response, successful firms are using the customer's perception of quality to set performance standards, rather than relying solely on operationally defined standards for service quality. They often conduct extensive research to determine the key elements that impact the customer's perception of service quality. When Ritz-Carlton won the Malcolm Baldrige National Quality Award, this was tangible evidence that paying careful attention to customers' service expectations can have a dramatic impact on the firm.

Expansion of leasing and rental businesses: The expansion of businesses that lease equipment and personnel to firms has been a contributing factor in the growth of the service sector. More and more firms are looking to outsource some elements of their operation, and they often start with elements that are not part of the firm's core product or business. For example, most hotels that host meetings and conventions have outsourced the servicing of the audiovisual needs of groups tc a company that specializes in that type of business. The company in turn leases the audiovisual equipment to groups that are holding meetings in the hotel. The company is able to provide more up-to-date and specialized equipment to groups than the hotel might if it provided the service itself. The hotel does not have to maintain an inventory of equipment, and therefore capital costs are reduced.

Manufacturers as service providers: Some of the firms that traditionally manufactured and distributed tangible products have found it profitable to provide services as well. For example, most automobile manufacturers have consumer credit agencies to facilitate the leasing and purchasing of automobiles. In the hospitality industry, PepsiCo decided to enter the restaurant industry and distribute its products through acquisitions such as Taco Bell and KFC, but the company later reconsidered this strategy and sold these brands to Yum! Brands, Inc. In the computer industry, firms such as IBM and Hewlett-Packard provide services in addition to hardware and software. In most cases, the profit margins on services are higher than on products, contributing significantly to the bottom line of the firm.

Pressures on public and nonprofit organizations to find new income sources: All organizations are under pressure to increase sales, which often becomes difficult within the traditional products that a firm sells. There are many reasons for this, but increasing competition and mature industries are often contributing factors. In an effort to find new sources of income, firms often seek new services that will generate new net sales, without cannibalizing sales of existing products. For example, a limousine company might expand its city tour business in addition to the other services offered.

Hiring and promotion of innovative managers: In the past, managers in the service industries often spent their entire careers within a single industry, or perhaps even with the same firm. This situation no longer re-mains the same, especially at the corporate level of management. Firms often hire individuals from other industries to provide a fresh perspective and fresh ideas. The results can become dramatic. One such individual is Steven Bollenback, president and CEO of Hilton Hotels. Prior to his very positive impact on Hilton Hotels, he had engineered innovative financing at both Marriott International and Trump Hotels and · Resorts.

Nature of Services

Along with the growth in services, an appreciation for the ways in which services are different from products has developed. The traditional ways of marketing tangible products are not equally effective in services marketing. In many industries, marketing involves tangible manufactured products, such as automobiles, washing machines, and clothing, whereas service industries focus on intangible products such as travel and foodservice. However, before we can explore how services get successfully marketed, we need to examine the ways services differ from products. Lovelock and Wright have identified nine key differences.

No ownership by customers: A customer does not take ownership when purchasing a service. There is no transfer of assets. Service products as intangible performers. The value of owning a highperformance car or the latest computer lies in the physical characteristics of the product and to some extent the brand image it conveys. The value of purchasing services lies in the nature of the performance. For example, if you decide to celebrate a birthday or anniversary by dining at an expensive restaurant, the value lies in the way in which the service actors perform. When servers come to the table and present all the entrees simultaneously, the choreographed presentation appears in the same manner as a choreographed play or performance.

Greater involvement of customers in the production process: Because consumers tend to be present when receiving service within a hospitality operation, they remain involved in the service production. In many instances, they are directly involved through the element of self-service. Examples of this can be seen in fast-food restaurants as well as in hotels that provide automated check-in and checkout by means of either a machine or a video connection through the television. Airlines have greatly expanded self-service within their operations as a means of reducing labor costs. In any case, the customer's level of satisfaction depends on the nature of the interaction with the service provider, the nature of the physical facilities in which the service gets provided, and the nature of the interaction with other guests present in the facility at the time the service is provided.

People as part of the product: People or firms that purchase services come in contact with other consumers as well as the service employees. For example, a hotel guest waits in line at the front desk or the concierge desk with other guests. In addition, the guests share facilities such as the pool, the restaurant, and the fitness center. Therefore, service firms must also manage consumer interactions to the best of their abilities to ensure customer satisfaction. For example, a hotel's sales office would not want to book group business with a nondrinking religious group at the same time as a reunion of military veterans. The two groups are significantly different in behavior, and the expectation is that they would not mix well within the facilities at the same time. Similarly, restaurants separate smokers and nonsmokers, and they should try to separate other patrons that show some potential for conflict.

Greater variability in operational inputs and outputs: In a manufacturing setting, the operational production can be controlled very carefully. For example, staff carefully manage inventory and precisely calculate production times. Services, however, are delivered in real time, with many variables not being fully under the control of managers. For example, if a guest has been promised an early check-in but all of the guests from the preceding night are late in checking out, it becomes more difficult for the hotel to honor the arriving guest's request.

A service setting remains a more difficult site in which to control quality and offer a consistent service experience. Service firms try to minimize the amount of variability between service encounters, but much of the final product stays situational. There are many uncontrollable aspects of the delivery process, such as weather, the number of consumers present, the attitudes of the consumers, and the attitudes of the employees. Therefore, it becomes impossible to consistently control the quality for services in the same manner as the quality of manufactured products.

Harder for consumers to evaluate: Consumers can receive considerable information regarding the purchase of products; however, they often do not obtain it for services. Prior to buying a product, a consumer can research the product attributes and performance and use this information when making a purchase decision, especially an important one.

No inventories for services: Due to the intangible nature of services, they cannot be inventoried for future use. Therefore, a lost sale can never be recaptured. When a seat remains empty on a flight, a hotel room stays vacant, or a table stays unoccupied in a restaurant, the potential revenue for these services at that point in time becomes lost forever. In other words, services are perishable, much like produce in a supermarket or items in a bakery. It remains critical for hospitality and tourism firms to manage supply and demand in an attempt to minimize unused capacity. For example, restaurants offer early-bird specials and airlines offer deeply discounted fares in an attempt to shift demand from peak periods to nonpeak periods, thereby increasing revenue and profits.

Importance of time: Hospitality services are generally produced and consumed simultaneously, unlike tangible products, which are manufactured, inventoried, and then sold at a later date. Customers must be present to receive the service. There are real limits to the amount of time that customers are willing to wait to receive service. Service firms study the phenomenon of service queues, or the maximum amount of time a customer will wait for a service before it has a significant (negative) impact on his or her perception of service quality. Airline companies offer curbside check-in for the most time-conscious passengers, and restaurants have devised practices such as providing guests with pagers and expanding the bar area in order to reduce the negative effect that results from waiting for service.

Different distribution channels: The distribution channel for services is usually more direct than the traditional channel (i.e., manufacturer-wholesalerretailer-consumer) used by many product firms. The simultaneous production and consumption normally associated with service delivery limits the use of intermediaries. The service firm usually comprises both the manufacturer and the retailer, with no need for a wholesaler to inventory its products. Consumers are present to consume the meals prepared in a restaurant, to take advantage of the amenities in a hotel, and to travel between cities by plane.

Behaviour of Consumers

When consumers make purchase decisions, they move

through a series of steps that explain the thought process leading up to and following the purchase of a product or service. Prior to making a purchase decision, consumers look for information about the product or service. Search qualities are attributes that the consumer can investigate prior to making a purchase. When purchasing hospitality and tourism services, consumers rely heavily on word of mouth and on promotional elements such as advertising and publicity. Since services are intangible, search qualities can be difficult to evaluate. However, advances in technology and the increase in consumer advocacy groups have resulted in more information being available to consumers prior to purchase.

The second set of qualities consumers use to evaluate services are experience qualities. These refer to the attributes that can be evaluated only after the purchase and consumption of a service. The intangible nature of services forces consumers to rely heavily on experience qualities in the final evaluation of services. Therefore, a high risk remains associated with the purchase of services. For example, consumers who want to purchase an automobile will test-drive the car and review and consult the consumer performance data that are available on that model. Conversely, consumers who rent cars cannot evaluate their purchases until after they have committed their payment. Few consumers will take the time or make the effort to test-drive potential rental cars prior to mak ing a decision at the time of rental. Similarly, consumers are taking a risk when they choose a restaurant because they cannot sample meals before they are purchased.

Finally, credence qualities are those attributes that are difficult to evaluate even after the service is consumed. Even though you arrive safely at your destination after a flight, you cannot evaluate the pilot's work in any real depth. In many cases, you know a service was not performed correctly only when an obvious mistake exists. For example, bacteria often appear on food served in restaurants, but the public becomes aware of it only when major ramifications such as food poisoning or deaths get publicized. Purchase decisions related to services are more difficult to make because of the lack of search qualities and the difficulty in evaluating credence qualities.

Consumers tend to rely on their own past experiences and those of others when making purchase decisions. Therefore, service firms must obtain as much feedback from consumers as possible. If consumers do not return, the firm may not know why, and the consumers will probably tell others about their experience. Service firms should know if consumers are not satisfied so that appropriate actions can be taken to improve the quality of service and increase repeat business.

Service Quality

Firms use two basic strategies to compete: become a low-cost provider of a particular service and focus on price competition, or focus on quality and try to differentiate your service from those offered by your competitors. Firms that can project high-quality images can charge higher prices. Service quality is a perception resulting from attitudes formed by customers' long-term, overall evaluations of performance. Service quality is affected by all of the individuals who have contact with customers. If one employee provides below-standard service or fails to satisfy the customer, a negative experience could result. Therefore, it is important to understand the entire process of service delivery that leads to consumer perceptions of quality.

The service quality process is the product of the expectations and perceptions of a firm's management, its employees, and the customers it serves. Whenever there are differences in expectations or perceptions between the people involved in the delivery and the consumption of services, a potential for a gap in service quality exists. Firms should diagnose any service quality gaps because there is a direct relationship between service quality and customer satisfaction. Simply stated, when customers are satisfied, they are much more likely to purchase from the service provider again. Over time, if they remain satisfied, they become loyal customers.

The service gap is the final gap that exists when there is a difference between customers' expectations of a service and their perceptions of the actual service once it is consumed. When this difference occurs, it is the result of one or more gaps that occur earlier in the service quality process. The first potential gap is referred to as the knowledge gap, which occurs when management's perception of what consumers expect is different from the consumers' actual expectations. This gap may lead to other gaps in the service quality process, and it is usually the result of a failure in the firm's research program or organizational structure. Firms need to obtain feedback from customers and employees that can be used to design services that will appeal to customers.

If the current service offering is not satisfying customers, then the firm should know from its customer surveys or because its employees are willing, and able, to provide valuable information that they obtain from customers, either voluntarily or involuntarily. The second potential gap is referred to as the standards gap, which refers to the discrepancy that can occur between management's perception of what customers expect and how the service delivery process is designed to meet those expectations. Management establishes the specifications to provide the desired service at the desired level of quality.

Therefore, even if management remains accurate in its perception of customer expectations, a gap could still exist in service because the delivery process does not accomplish the goals of the firm. For example, management may have correctly determined the amount of time that customers are willing to wait to check in to a hotel, but they may not schedule enough front desk clerks to meet the customers' expectations. This could result from a lack of commitment on the part of management or the result of management trying to reduce the firm's operating costs.

One of the techniques used by management is to develop a service blueprint -a flow chart that details the delivery process, including the points of contact with customers. This will help to uncover any shortcomings in the delivery process that may lead to a gap in service quality. Management should document each step in the process to identify areas for improvement. The third potential gap is referred to as the delivery gap, which occurs when there is a difference between the service delivery specifications and the actual service delivery.

Management may have correctly assessed customer expectations and developed specifications that will meet these expectations, but employees may not deliver the service properly. For example, a restaurant may specify that wait staff should approach customers within two minutes of seating. However, the wait staff may stand around discussing their plans for later in the evening and ignoring the specifications. Firms must find ways to create an atmosphere for employees that ensures their willingness to perform the job tasks as desired by management.

Employee selection and training are critical in this process, as are the rewards and recognition provided for good performance. The fourth potential gap is referred to as the communications gap, which occurs when there is a difference between the service delivered and the service promised through the firm's external communications with customers.

Many firms have a tendency to promise more than they can deliver in an attempt to persuade customers. For instance, advertisements for hospitality and tourism firms lead customers to believe that in the event of a problem or mishap the firms will do whatever they can to satisfy customers. Making promises to consumers that cannot be delivered is a big mistake that service providers often make. It results in service performance levels that are below consumer expectations, leading to dissatisfaction. Each individual consumer makes purchase decisions and has established, based on past experiences, a set of expectations for the performance of a product or service.

Anyone who travels on a regular basis can provide stories related to experiences with airlines, hotels, and restaurants. Ironically, firms that advertise 100 percent satisfaction guarantees are banking on the fact that most customers will not complain or force the issue. In other cases, firms simply neglect to inform customers about procedures or policies that would affect their expectations. For example, a good waitress will make sure that customers know that a dish is spicy or that a certain entrée will take longer to properly prepare, so that customers can make informed decisions and are less likely to become dissatisfied, because the actual performance will more closely match consumer expectations.

If any of the first four gaps occur, then the service gap will occur because the actual service will not meet the customer's expectations. Comment cards and basic surveys will often uncover a service gap, but they may lack the detail needed to evaluate the other potential gaps. Therefore, firms should have a mechanism in place to obtain feedback from customers and employees that can be used to examine the entire service quality process. If services do not meet customers' expectations of quality, then the customers become dissatisfied and will likely not return. Also, they will convey these negative experiences to their friends and colleagues.

Management

To provide high-quality service, all members of the staff,

from the highest to the lowest level on the organizational chart, must view the guest as the highest priority. Delivering high-quality service is based on an attitude of serving customers. Developing an attitude that places the customer as the highest priority for the business remains critical. Without satisfied customers and repeat patron- age, the business will not succeed in the long term. To develop a servicequality orientation, customers should be perceived in the following way:

— Each customer is the most important person in any business.
— Customers are not dependent on us, but we are dependent on them.
— Customers do not interrupt our work. They are the purpose for it.
— Customers do us a favor when they call. We are not doing them favors by providing them services.
— Customers are part of our business, not outsiders.
— Customers are human beings like us, with the same feelings and emotions.
— Customers bring us their wants, and it is our job to fulfill them.
— Customers deserve the most courteous and attentive service we can provide.
— Customers are the lifeblood of every business.

Firms that use a customer orientation become more successful at providing products and services that meet customers' needs and expectations. In contrast, firms that assume they know what is best for the customer are more likely to fail. This is further illustrated by those firms that successfully engage in relationship and internal marketing.

Relationship Marketing: All progressive companies devote marketing resources to attract and retain new customers. Relationship marketing is based on the proposition that it is less expensive to keep the customers you already have than to acquire new customers. It is shortsighted to think that merely attracting new customers will keep the business headed in a successful direction. Rather, an equal amount of attention and resources should be devoted to keeping the customer base that already exists. In times of slow market growth and increasing competition, it will be less expensive to maintain an existing customer base than to seek new customers.

Relationship marketing involves attracting, developing, and retaining customer relationships. This long-term view toward the customer must be seen as being equal in importance to attracting new customers. Many firms make the mistake of focusing on new customers at the expense of existing customers, and the level of service quality diminishes. For example, hotel sales managers are expected to develop new accounts with corporate and association groups. Sometimes they spend so much time trying to get these new accounts that they neglect some of their existing accounts. This lack of attention may cost the hotel the group's future business because they took the customer for granted. Service firms should build relationships and maintain them. A relationship marketing approach is highly desirable upon meeting the following conditions:

— A customer has an ongoing or periodic desire for the service.

— The service customer controls the selection of the service organization.

— Alternative service providers make it easy for customers to switch.

All three of these conditions are present in the hospitality and tourism industry. Many firms offer special prices and additional services to highly desirable customers in an attempt to build long-term relationships. These practices are most commonly used with business accounts and frequent users. For example, hotels provide contract rates for corporations that supply a high volume of annual business. Airlines receive one of the lowest rates possible in hotels near airports because they have flight crews who need guest rooms on a daily basis. Also, airlines build relationships with frequent flyers by providing them with additional services such as preboarding, free upgrades, and airport clubs where they can rest or conduct business away from crowded lounges at departure gates.

Internal Marketing: In addition to focusing efforts on consumers, firms can achieve higher levels of service quality by marketing to their employees. Internal marketing encompasses all activities used by a firm in an effort to improve the marketing effectiveness of its employees. Efforts should be made to communicate with all employees, especially those in boundaryspanning roles who come in contact with customers. The ability to deliver consistent, high-quality service depends on the organization's ability to recruit, train, retain, and motivate dedicated service personnel.

First, service firms need to select and hire employees who are willing and able to provide high-quality service. There are many people in the job market, and firms need to create attractive positions that appeal to highly motivated individuals. A range of potential service exists that an employee can provide from the minimum necessary to retain the position and not be penalized to the maximum possible service. This variability in the level of possible service is referred to as discretionary effort. For example, if an airline passenger leaves a carry-on item on a flight, the airline's personnel have some discretion as to the level of service they will provide. They can take their time and forward the item to the traveler's next destination, or they can try to deliver it to the traveler before he or she boards the next plane or leaves the airport.

Second, service firms should provide employees with adequate training so they possess the skills that are required in performing their job tasks. In addition, the firm should communicate with employees so they are aware of changes within the organization as well as upcoming events. If service personnel are well trained and they understand what management expects, the environment is right for success. Firms can use both internal communications, such as newsletters and e-mail, and external communications, such as advertising and public relations, to convey their expectations to employees.

An advertisement can be used to create and manage consumer perceptions and expectations, but at the same time, the ad can be used to educate employees as well. One of the major airlines aired a commercial on television that showed an athletic employee running through the airport to catch a traveler who left his briefcase at the check-in counter. This commercial served two purposes: (1) it let customers know that the airline provided high-quality service, and (2) it gave employees an idea of the firm's service expectations. Finally, firms need to provide employees with rewards and recognition when they perform at a high level of discretionary effort. This motivates service providers to continue performing at high levels and to remain loyal to the firm.

Retaining good employees is important in providing high-quality service, and it reduces the costs associated with turnover. It takes a great deal of time and effort to hire and train good employees. Firms can use extrinsic rewards such as salary increases and bonuses or intrinsic rewards such as recognition and job satisfaction to motivate employees. Many firms recognize "employees of the month" by honoring them with plaques displayed where customers can see them or allowing them to use special parking spaces close to the building.

Importance of Customer Satisfaction

Most firms understand the importance of customer satisfaction and will provide basic training to their employees. The more sophisticated firms actually have instruments that they use to measure customer satisfaction and establish benchmarks for future comparisons. Benchmarking is a process whereby a firm establishes a level of performance by comparing current performance against past performance, or by comparing current performance against the performance of other companies or an entire industry. Data are used to create benchmarks, which then become the standard against which current and future performance is evaluated. Unfortunately, many firms still only pay lip service to customer satisfaction and the complaints received from customers. The following information was collected through the efforts of the Technical Assistance Research Program in the 1980s, but it remains accurate today:

— The average business does not hear from 96 percent of its unhappy customers.

— For every complaint received, 26 other customers have the same problem.

— The average person with a problem tells 9 or 10 people, and 13 percent will tell more than 20.

— Customers who have their complaints resolved to their satisfaction tell an average of 5 people about the experience.

— Complainers are more likely to do business with you again than noncomplainers who have a problem: 54-70 percent if resolved, and 95 percent if resolved quickly.

These statistics support the contention that a dissatisfied customer tells people about a bad experience more often than a satisfied customer tells people about a good experience. However, firms should take note that it is beneficial to have customers voice their complaints so that they can be resolved and increase the likelihood that the customers will return.

Improving customer service should be a top priority of all managers working in the hospitality and tourism industry. Customer satisfaction occurs when a firm's service, as perceived by customers, meets or exceeds expectations. Firms that can consistently meet or exceed customer expectations will develop good reputations and often good quality images. When we travel, we encounter service providers in hotels and restaurants who provide exceptional service. This type and consistency of service does not happen by accident; it begins with a commitment by management to make it that way. Conversely, when the opposite occurs, the finger should be pointed at management as well.

Following are the five steps to improving customer service.

Define your standards of quality service with measurable indicators. Before you can evaluate the level of service provided by employees within your organization, you must establish the standards by which they will be judged. These standards, or benchmarks, should be observable and measurable. For example, it might be reasonable to expect front desk agents to answer the telephone within four rings or room service to deliver meals within 30 minutes of when the order was received. Once these standards are developed, they must be communicated to all personnel. It remains crucial that standards be clearly defined before any plans are developed to improve the level of service.

There are two major dimensions to define quality service: the procedural dimension and the convivial dimension. The procedural dimension includes incremental flow of service, timeliness, accommodating consumer needs, anticipating consumer needs before they occur or are requested by the consumer, communicating in a clear and concise manner, obtaining consumer feedback, and coordinating through proper supervision. The convivial dimension includes displaying a positive attitude and body language, using the guest's name as a means of delivering personal attention, attending to the guest on a personal basis, providing guidance to guests who are indecisive, and solving problems that arise.

Assess your current situation: As in any continuous improvement program, before you move forward, you must determine your current position. This can be done by objectively assessing the level of service currently provided within the organization; this involves conducting an audit of the services provided by service personnel within the organization. As a result of the audit, the strengths and weaknesses of the firm can be determined; this will provide a means of building on the aspects of service that are positive and improving the areas that are deficient. Audits can be conducted using mystery shoppers, or corporations may use staff members to audit the performance of units within the company.

Develop effective service improvement strategies: This must be accomplished through well-planned and thorough training of service providers. Attention must be paid to identifying objectives for the training and providing specific instructions and clear descriptions of the expected outcomes of the training.

Initiate your solutions carefully: As with any plan, implementation is the most critical stage. You should proceed with caution, taking steps incrementally rather than all at once. You should build on small successes, rather than trying to accomplish too much too soon.

Provide feedback, recognition, and rewards: Positive feedback must be provided if the change in behavior continues. A reward structure must be provided that will maintain the level of interest and enthusiasm among the service providers throughout their careers. This represents a major challenge for management, but one that is well worth the effort. Finally, management must continually evaluate the performance of its employees and make the appropriate changes. Over time, customers' expectations of service firms change, and competitive firms may increase the level of service that is considered the standard in an industry. Therefore, firms must constantly reassess their strategies and redefine their service standards. Service performance and customer satisfaction should be measured and evaluated using benchmarks established during previous periods. Also, direct comparisons with the performance of firms considered industry leaders are an excellent way to establish goals for future improvement.

Failure of Management

Service failures occur at critical incidents, or "moments of truth," in the service encounter, when customers interact with a firm's employees. It is important to provide service personnel with the authority and the recovery tools necessary to correct service failures as they occur. In this section we can see different types of service failures, common consumer complaints, and recovery strategies that can be used to repair the service failures.

Service failures

The timeliness and form of response by service providers to service failures will have a direct impact on customer satisfaction and quality perceptions. Service failures are assigned to one of three major categories:

— responses to service delivery system failures,

— responses to customer needs and requests, and

— unprompted and unsolicited employee actions.

The first category, system failures, refers to failures in the core service offering of the firm. These failures are the result of normally available services being unavailable, unreasonably slow service, or some other core service failure that will differ by industry. For example, a hotel's pool may have a leak and be closed, a customer may have to wait a long time for the shuttle to an airport car rental agency, or an airline might mishandle a passenger's luggage.

The second category, customer needs failures, are based on employee responses to customer needs or special requests. These failures come in the form of special needs, customer preferences, customer errors, and disruptive others (i.e., disputes between customers). For example, a hotel guest may want to have a pet in the room, a customer may want to be switched to an aisle seat on an airplane, a customer at an event may lose his ticket, or a customer in a restaurant may be smoking in a nonsmoking section.

The third category, unsolicited employee actions, refers to the actions, both good and bad, of employees that are not expected by customers. These actions can be related to the level of attention an employee gives to customers, to unusual actions that can be performed by employees, to an action's reinforcement of a customer's cultural norms, or to an employee's actions under adverse conditions. For example, a hostess in a restaurant could anticipate the needs of a family with a small child, a hotel front desk clerk could give a free upgrade to a guest who waited in line too long, a flight attendant could ignore passengers with children, or a cruise ship employee could help to evacuate passengers during a crisis.

Consumer complaints

Certain undesired outcomes are associated with dissatisfied customers. Two of the most common are to engage in negative word of mouth and to change service providers. A third, less common reaction is to engage in some form of retaliation. This retaliation can range from a negative word-of-mouth campaign to causing physical damage or launching a major protest. The way a firm approaches and handles complaints will determine its long-term performance. Some firms show a dislike for customers who complain, while other firms create an atmosphere that encourages customers to voice their concerns. For example, Bertucci's Brick Oven Pizzerias, headquartered in Massachusetts, offers customers a tollfree number that they can call to register a complaint. One of the primary reasons for doing this is to provide dissatisfied customers with an outlet to have their concerns heard and to take immediate steps to resolve the complaint. By doing so, the firm hopes to reduce negative word of mouth and to retain customers.

Most customers complain in an attempt to reverse an undesirable state. Other more complicated reasons for complaining are to release pressure, to regain some form of control over a situation, or to get the sympathy of others. Whatever the reason, the outcome is that customers are not completely satisfied, and it is in the firm's best interest to know when this occurs. There are many other dissatisfied customers who do not complain because they don't know what to do or they don't think it will do any good.

Service recovery strategies

When customers complain, firms are presented with the opportunity to recover from service failures. Recovery strategies, and actions occur when a firm's reaction to a service failure results in customer satisfaction and goodwill. In fact, customers who are involved in successful service recoveries often demonstrate higher levels of satisfaction than customers who do not report service failures or complain. The following list describes popular service recovery strategies:

Cost/benefit analysis: Service firms should compare the costs of losing customers and obtaining new customers with the benefits of keeping existing customers. Most firms place a high value on retaining customers. However, some guests take advantage of satisfaction guarantees and complain on every occasion. Many hotel chains, such as Doubletree, maintain a database on complaints and will flag chronic complainers.

Actively encourage complaints: It is better to know when customers are not satisfied so that action can be taken to rectify the situation. It is im-portant to note that while unhappy customers may not complain to service firms, they will often complain to their family and friends. Hospitality and tourism firms use comment cards and toll-free numbers to encourage customers to provide feedback. Also, service personnel are trained to ask customers whether everything was satisfactory.

Anticipate the need for recovery: Service firms should "blueprint" the service delivery process and determine the moments of truth, or critical incidents, where customers interact with employees. The process can be designed to avoid failures, but recovery plans should be established for use in the event that a failure occurs.

Respond quickly: The timelier the response in the event of a service failure, the more likely that recovery efforts will be successful. Once a customer leaves a service establishment, the likelihood of a successful recovery falls dramatically. Based on this principle, firms such as Marriott International provide service hotlines at each hotel to help resolve problems quickly. Managers and associates know that the speed with which they respond is often as critical as what the final resolution becomes.

Train employees: Employees should be informed of the critical incidents and provided with potential strategies for recovery. For example, some hotel training programs use videotaped scenarios of service failures to show employees potential problems and the appropriate solutions.

Empower the front line: In many cases, a successful recovery will hinge on a frontline employee's ability to take timely action and make a decision. Firms should empower employees to handle service failures at the time they occur, within certain limits. For example, Ritz-Carlton allows its employees to spend up to $1,000 to take care of dissatisfied customers. One of the classic examples of a service failure involved Northwest Airlines during a major winter storm at the Detroit airport. Unfortunately, due to the heavy snow, many outbound flights were canceled, and no gates were available for unloading passengers from the inbound flights.

This traffic jam left many passengers stranded as the airplanes sat on the taxiways for as long as eight hours. Northwest's inability to provide the passengers with information or a solution resulted in hundreds of unhappy passengers and a class action lawsuit. Having delayed flights and a shortage of gates is not a new phenomenon at airports in climates such as Detroit's, and Northwest Airlines should have had a viable service recovery program in place that could have lessened the severity of the problem.

Techniques Used for Assess Customer Satisfaction

One of the critical components of a firm's commitment to customer satisfaction is feedback that provides an assessment of the firm's performance. Then benchmarks can be established and future progress can be evaluated. Also, these measures can be used to reward service personnel in a way that stays consistent with a firm's customer satisfaction goals. The following section describes the most common techniques used by firms to assess customer satisfaction.

Spoken Comments and Complaints: Listening to consumer comments and complaints remains the most straightforward way to evaluate customer satisfaction. Service firms should set up formal systems that encourage customer and employee feedback regarding service experiences. Management should not overlook the value of the information obtained by boundary-spanning personnel through their normal contact with customers. One of the most recent approaches is providing toll-free numbers so that customers can call to voice complaints.

Surveys and Comment Cards: Many hospitality and tourism firms leave comment cards in guest rooms, on tables in restaurants, and at other points of contact so that they can obtain feedback. One of the problems associated with this method is the lack of representation. The response rate is small, and it tends to be biased toward those who are most upset and chronic complainers. Larger operations will conduct surveys through the corporate offices by either telephone or mail. Surveys will normally be more representative than comment cards and provide more detailed information. These types of surveys also provide for a more representative sample of customers.

Number of Repeat Customer: Service firms can gauge customer satisfaction by keeping track of repeat business. Higher levels of satisfaction would be associated with higher percentages of repeat customers. This models an unobtrusive method of assessing customer satisfaction, but it does not provide much detail.

Trends in Sales and Market Share: Another way to evaluate customer satisfaction without direct contact with customers is to examine the firm's internal sales records. Comparisons can be made on a month-to-month basis and with the same period of the previous year. Higher levels of satisfaction would be associated with increases in sales. However, firms should be careful with this method because there are many possible explanations for increases in sales. For example, the firm may have launched a new advertising campaign, a competitor may be renovating or going out of business, or the firm may have decreased its prices. In addition to examining sales records, firms should also look at market share. This measure considers sales in relation to the competition, which is a more accurate assessment of improved market performance. However, there could also be other explanations for changes in market share besides customer satisfaction.

Shopping Reports: Another approach used by hospitality and tourism firms involves having someone consume a service just like any other customer. The "secret shopper" can be an employee of the firm, an outside person chosen by the firm, or an employee of an outside firm that specializes in this service assessment activity. These shoppers are normally equipped with detailed evaluation forms based on company guidelines that can be used to record the desired information. It is often recommended that someone outside the firm be used in an attempt to maintain some level of objectivity. It is important to have a particular operation evaluated by more than one shopper on several occasions throughout the desired period. Doing so will result in a more representative sample of service experiences.

Several Issues and Trends

Identifying trends within any business is one of the keys to success. Being in a position to identify what is occurring and what is likely to occur in the future remains very important. When studying trends in a broad sense, one should examine five major areas: the competitive environment, the economic environment, the political and legal environment, the social environment, and the technological environment.

Several issues and trends are critical to understanding hospitality and tourism marketing. They help put into proper perspective what occurs within the competitive marketplace. Three trends that are having an impact on the hospitality industry and will continue to do so are shrinking customer loyalty, increasing customer sophistication, and increasing emphasis on the needs of individual customers.

Shrinking customer loyalty

Advertising and promotion for the hospitality and tourism industry's product-service mix have traditionally focused on the product, the services provided, and the physical plant or atmosphere in which the customer enjoys the product-service mix. Today, many hospitality and tourism firms focus their promotions on price; that is, heavy price competition exists along with a good deal of discounting. Unfortunately, price discounting exists as a short-term strategy that seldom builds brand loyalty. Consumers often shop around for the best deal and are loyal only to organizations that give them a consistently superior one. Recognizing this, companies have sought ways to increase brand loyalty, especially among heavy users of the productservice mix.

The best examples of this approach are the frequent flyer programs promoted by the airlines and the frequent traveler programs promoted by the lodging companies. These loyalty programs are commonplace in the lodging industry; all of the major chains use loyalty programs to encourage and reward frequent guests. The strategy behind loyalty programs is to hook the customer with points which can be redeemed for products or services. The more frequently the customer stays at a hotel operated by the company, the more points are earned. The basic concepts common to all of these programs are:

— Identify individuals who frequently purchase your product-service mix.

— Recognize the contribution those individuals make to the success of your company.

— Reward those individuals with awards and incentives that will increase their loyalty to your company and its brands.

Tie-ins with other companies providing travel-related services are also frequently used. For example, airlines, hotels, and car rental companies frequently offer bonus points within their programs if the traveler uses the services offered by one of the companies participating in the tie-in. Both the airlines and the hotel companies are constantly making minor alterations to their programs.

Increasing consumer sophistication

The budget segment of the lodging industry has undergone significant growth in the last several years. This growth has been fueled by the consumer demand for affordable accommodations that provide good value. In fact, consumers focus more on value and less on quality or price alone. Consumers have become more sophisticated and understand the concept of value at any price level. Companies have responded with brands that offer good quality at an affordable price. Each of these brands features nicely appointed guest rooms, limited or no public meeting space, limited or no food service provided on the hotel site, and a complimentary continental breakfast for guests. These limited-service brands incur lower development and operating expenses and thereby can provide guests with a lower price and good value, something that all consumers are seeking.

Hotels in the upscale segment are also trying to increase the consumer's perception of value. They continually provide a broad assortment of amenities, such as health clubs on the property, business centers, rooms that provide more work space for business travelers, and personalized concierge service. These properties are striving to become "one-stop" destinations, providing a complete product-service mix that includes many food and beverage outlets, in-house office services, a wide variety of meeting room configurations, and other services, such as recreation, that will appeal to potential guests.

Within the fast-food service segment, companies often "bundle" their products in an attempt to increase sales and provide a better value for their customers. For example, they combine a sandwich, a large order of french fries, and a large soft drink at a price lower than what the items would cost if purchased separately. Similarly, tour operators and travel agents attempt to provide customers with more value by "bundling" the various components of travel at a price lower than the sum of the individual components. This approach is known as product bundling.

Increased emphasis on the needs of individual customers

The markets within both hospitality and tourism segments have been segmented for a long time. In the past 5 to 15 years, this trend has become even more pronounced. Mass marketing has become a thing of the past as more firms extend their product lines to meet the specific needs of smaller segments of travelers and diners. This phenomenon has become most apparent in the lodging industry. During the last decade, most of the major lodging chains developed several new brands or types of lodging properties to appeal to market segments that they were not currently serving. In addition, many hotel chains have merged with or acquired other hotel chains that focus on different market segments.

Improvements in technology have given firms the ability to maintain large databases that detail consumer purchasing behavior and preferences. This information can be used to direct marketing efforts toward individual customers or market segments. Instead of relying on the mass media for promotions, a marketer can target past customers through direct mail and e-mail with special promotions and incentives that have a higher probability of being successful. There is more customization of products and promotions and less wasted coverage with media campaigns.

5

Destination Marketing

The worldwide travel industry is changing at an unprecedented rate, there is an increasing trend towards more independent travel, more short breaks, more vacations. There are a growing number of destinations and products for consumers to choose from. Consumers need more information, more quickly and they need to be able to book easily, and with a quality of service they received elsewhere in their purchasing. Destination Marketing Systems offer a solution to these problems. They are not perfect but are an emerging phenomenon that are worthwhile for tourist boards to evaluate seriously - especially those that attract high numbers of independent travellers.

As the most valuable asset of a destination is the local people with its hospitality, and with its way how to approach the visiting guests, the modern communication society is a new determinative element to define tourism policies and strategies. The sustainable coherence of a destination widely depends on the well balanced and true infor-mation sharholders, stakeholders, and customers. This is the most efficient way to build up a sound public opinion for the cause of tourism. Unfortunately, the media are not always handling this game properly as they have a tendency to be just the voice of the consumer instead of being also the advocate of the stringent socio-economic factors of tourism.

Despite the fact that among decision makers worldwide there is an increasing awareness that tourism is a superior consumer good which would deserve a much bigger investment for maketing purposes as the stake for promotion compared to the overall turnover is merely 4%. To give you an example: Watchmakers at the high end of quality have to invest up to 25% for promotion in order to defend their marketshare. Due to the shortfall of public funds the private sector as well the National, Regional and Local Tourist Boards are under heavy presure from Governments to take a bigger financial burden for destination marketing and for greater focus on core tasks. However, it is our responsibility to set the points in a way that the interests of both the private and public stakeholdes will evolve even more towards partnership instead towards conflict, i.e. we have to generate win-win situations.

It is quite conceivable to regard tourism as a kind of theatrical performance that is played out on a stage called "Destination", but in a relationship between host and visitor that pays regard to human dignity and the cultural identity of the hosts. Nevertheless, the question must be asked: is there sufficient recognition of the fact by both the industry and the public sector that they are condemned to partnership? With regard to sustainability, will they have the courage to move on from lip-service declarations to confront the moment of truth for tourism? If we wish to achieve the strategic goals of sustainability, we must first define the role of the relevant indicators that must be found at the economic, social and environmental levels. As time passes, the careful and wise use of the natural environment is becoming the key factor for the attractiveness of tourism destinations of all sorts..

In the 21st century, we who work in tourism must find a clearly defined policy of "qualitative growth". This means that we must again recognise that the capital assets of tourism consist of elements that are easily destroyed, namely our human capital, our culture, nature and the environment. We must learn to use these assets - but not to use them up! Tourism can only generate stable employment if the environment is tolerable for the local inhabitant and the visitor alike.

We should welcome the warnings of "devil's advocates" who say that sustainability is a long-term concept which creates added value by the law of the optimisation and not the maximisation of income, that is to say, it does not want the hen to lay the eggs, and at the same time to be served up on a plate as a fried chicken. A destination's volume share of tourism demand is not so important as its share of the worldwide potential of good and cultured visitors who realize that a good product cannot be acquired at a dumping price. Mass tourism has been described as the "occupation of a country by an unarmed army for a limited period of time" This is the image of tourism that we must combat: quality of offer and quality of demand, permanently monitored, must be the tourism which we have to strive for. Therefore every destination should establish ethical guidlines in order to satisfy the legitimate needs of both the host and the guestside.

"Tourism is not one but all industries", This indicates not only tourism's high multiplication factor but also that tourism is the substratum of many policies - economic, regional, local, social and cultural. Not everything that seems to be profitable to the individual businessman is desirable for the overall economy. Shareholder value taken to the extreme is poison for the social coherence of a society, and is the cultivation of mere egoism. What does this mean in relation to tourism? It is in fact an emanation of history and culture, and one of its vehicles of transmission, we link a new ethos for tourism to the following hope in the form of a realistic vision:

— The relationship between supplier and consumer must change to a partnership with parallel interests. In this way it will be possible to arouse support on both sides for genuine sustainablity and to convert exagerated hedonism into a rational pleasure in consumption. The interests of shareholders and stakeholders must not conflict, but be complementary.

— Tourism should not only talk of the visitors' rights but also of their duties.Friendliness is not just something to be expected from the host. Visitors too should show more respect for the other peoples' otherness and other identiy. "Every guest is a king - but every king is just a guest".

— Development policies for tourism should be discussed from the start with the local population, so that they too support them. The representatives of hospitality are not just the professionals, but the whole population. This will avoid tourism becoming a ghetto culture.

— The social standing and the conditions of employment of the labour in the tourist sector must be improved.

The development of the relationship between the private and public sector at all destinations' levels has generated new laws, e.g. creating residental taxes or increasing those already in existence. Particular activities have detached and privatised, and much more. However, it is more creative and inno-vative to stengthen public-private partnership, and even more important to stimulate coherent Destination Marketing Policies Benchmarking and Branding than to set up too narrow a network of bureaucracy.

There are however limits of feasibility as it is not easy to draw the line between public and private players, whilst on the other hand pressure from the authorities on tourist administrations at all levels makes their taking action more difficult. The will to adapt to changed market and political conditions is certainly there, but the implementation creates problems. There is little difficulty in quantifying the activity of a tourism board carried out for the benefit of the private stakeholder so that it can serve as the basis of its financial performance.

These are all the basic activities that make .economically directed marketing subsequently possible. It is clear to everyone that it would be senselessto make the financing of basic research at universities dependent on an immediate econo-mic return on investment. The same criterion however is also valid for destination marketing carried out by tourist boards. Their task is becoming all the more difficult because the ethical basis of tourism is affected by the wide-spread obsession with shareholder value. Where, however, there is no understanding for long-term interests, where strategic thinking is replaced by day-to-day hectic tactical manoeuvering, there can be not true sustainability.

As keepers of the destination 'brand', tourist boards are responsible for positioning the destination in the minds of the consumer. This usually involves expensive print or broadcast media campaigns, often with no call to action and only sometimes with a number to call for brochure fulfillment. These enquiries are rarely tracked and almost never followed up, as the fulfillment of the brochure request is generally an isolated act, often executed by a third party, which is not connected, physically or philosophically, to any other component of the marketing chain. The tourism marketing chain is given below:

Awareness—Information—Booking—On-trip services—
Post-trip relationship.

At another point in the chain are reservations or selling systems. Examples of these would be, in the private sector, the airline GDS, and in the public sector destination systems like Gulliver in Ireland. Neither system really 'sells': the GDS are primarily productivity tools for travel agents to sell airline seats. Information on destination systems can be hard to access and the ability to book is usually limited to the suppliers who have paid to be listed.

Systems like Gulliver, while containing a reasonable selection of accommodation, are generally only accessible once the traveller has reached the destination, limiting the potential only to service clients who have already chosen their holiday or are on an inexpensive, book-as-you-go B&B tour. There is little evidence that such systems are any more than expensive booking substitutes, not generating any incremental business.

Table 1. Successful and failed systems

Features associated with successful systems	Features associated with Failed systems
Comprehensive database	Incomplete database
High quality, accurate, reliable information	Out of date, inaccurate data
Targeted at independent travellers	Seen to compete with the travel trade
Effective call centre operation	Difficult to book
Supported and promoted by tourist boards	Support withdrawn or withheld by tourist boards
Complementary to existing channels of distribution	Compete with existing channels of distribution
Run by marketing driven organisations	Run by bureaucratic organisations
Technology supports marketing	Driven by technology
Design products by listening to the customer	Simply provide lists of product with no packaging

Quality of Tourism

In this section we can see integrated information, destination marketing and reservation systems as Destination Marketing Systems (DMS). They, or parts of them, may be referred to elsewhere as Destination Databases or Destination Management Systems. On the demand side they cater for multiple forms of access by potential visitors - directly or through travel agents and tour operators, to call-centres, visitor information centres and the like and increasingly by distribution through airline GDS, home shopping networks (both on TV and computer) and the Internet. Potential visitors can be logged into a client database and tracked through their purchase life-cycle.

There is clear value to the private sector in access to targeted information about potential and actual visitors to a destination. Some tourist boards face legislation which restricts their ability to market this information to the private sector. Outsourcing of the destination marketing system may be one method of circumventing this. Destinations have been slow to follow the successful trends of affinity marketing and the creation of frequent flyer/ visitor programs in the private sector of the travel industry. This is a clear opportunity for the private and public sector to work together. By storing information about enquiries and any bookings the tourist board is able to measure its marketing effectiveness clearly-an option not easily open to it without DMS.

On the supply side DMS provide a comprehensive database of products and services that the destination has to offer. Destinations developing products and services databases today need to be aware of the many changes in distribution technology, and the rapid introduction of multimedia, and include the ability to store text, still and moving images and sound in their database.

International Initiatives

Effective information systems tend to be publicly funded, such as TIS, in the Tyrol, Austria. Effective reservation systems tend to come from the private sector. Initiatives to widen the scope of existing public sector reservation or information systems or to develop full destination marketing systems have only recently been commenced. Indeed to date there have been more examples of failed initiatives than successes. Failures have occurred at the planning stage as well as at the operational and all add to the learning curve, much of which is related to the relationship between the private and public sector, and conflicts, or perceived conflicts, between sales direct to the consumer and through the travel industry.

Destination Marketing System-Check in, Nova Scotia

The Ministry of Tourism in Nova Scotia has been successfully running a reservation service for 15 years. The system currently generates 300,000 inquiry calls per year, and makes 70,000 reservations for the 700 registered properties. Over 30 per cent of the business is generated from the USA and 17 per cent, again mostly from the USA, comes through travel agents. However, in 1993 it was decided that in the future it would be more profitable for the private sector to take control of the organisation. At the same time its current information and reservation system needed replacement. Following a tender process the business was won by the CCL group in Nova Scotia, who partnered SHL Systemhouse, Canada's largest system integrator, in choosing Infocentre's infoRMTM system as the natural successor to the previous system.

A new organisation CorporaTel-was established employing many of the existing tourism staff. The system enables the province to track customers through the entire contact/sales cycle, by building a client data base and then using the information in outbound marketing. Nova Scotia is looking to the new system to help it develop additional services for the consumer, the travel trade and its own tourism industry. It aims to help consumers and the travel trade with travel decisions and arrangements as well as motivating them to spend more time in Nova Scotia. Since the new agreement responses have increased- reservations are up 35 per cent - while call costs are down. The new system acts as the central source for up to-date travel information, which is retrievable in a combination of key words. The product database contains wide range of bookable service throughout the province.1

A failed Destination Marketing System-Bravo, UK

Bravo started as a concept, initiated by the British Tourist Authority, for an industry owned switch to connect suppliers and customers. However, the private sector refused to invest in speculative long-term project, without control. A lack of public funds to develop the system resulted in the concept being taken over by a group of private sector companies who changed strategy and technology several time over the course of a couple of years. The companies did not have a good grasp of the marketplace, alienated the public and private sector and only signed up 300 accommodation providers before the company failed.

Call Centres

A call centre offers the opportunity to bring the consumer and supplier closer together, to create a unified shopfront for tourism in the destination. The call centre will have access to the wide range of tourism accommodation in the destination, from the five star hotels through B&Bs and even campus grounds. A well-run operation will have instant access to availability either through freesell, inventory, or on-line connection to the accommodation providers. It offers an opportunity for the small accommodation providers to reach a greater marketplace cost-effectively. This is particularly attractive where major destinations, such as Scotland and Ireland, comprise thousands of small individual properties, rather than a destination such as

Hong Kong which has a smaller number of larger hotels-with existing distribution mechanisms in place. In addition to simple accommodation requests a call centre can offer trip design and packaging capabilities.

Distribution of Tourism Related Information

There are an increasing range of options for the distribution of tourism related information, both through the travel industry and direct to the consumer. The subject of distribution could easily fill an entire article on its own but it is interesting to note that the GDS have failed to provide the travel industry with effective distribution tools for leisure products. Countries outside of North America, where there is highly developed leisure travel, such as Germany and the UK, have developed their own networks, outside of the GDS, for distribution of leisure products, largely from tour operators, to the travel trade. Distribution direct to consumers is in its infancy.

Private networks such as CompuServe and Prodigy have already achieved a degree of success in North America, where local call access is free unlike many other parts of the world. These private networks are currently being dwarfed by the Internet, essentially an unmonitored publicly funded network, which is growing at a staggering rate of approximately one million users per month. It now has 30 million users, of whom three to four million are consumers, rather than academics or other users for work purposes. This growth is placing great stresses on the system, added to by the private networks who provide Internet access to their users. There are currently many travel and tourism initiatives on the Internet. However, it is likely in the long term that private networks, such as the about-to-be-launched Microsoft Network, will provide the most effective consumer distribution, along with interactive television.

Print media is under threat from multimedia. Tourist boards are targets for the ever increasing number of multimedia companies. These companies have a need to demonstrate the attraction of their products, such as CD-ROM's, to potential customers and other information providers. Tourism is an attractive target for them - lots of available pictures and information. Often they will offer tourist boards completely free manufacture of CD-ROM's in order to build a product portfolio, in exchange for the tourist board providing the information. The challenge for the multimedia company is distribution - does the company have guaranteed distribution to the travel industry or potential travellers? The challenge to the tourist board is ensuring that they own a product database that is capable of storing multimedia data - text, photographs and even sound and video clips.

Finance, Organisation and Operation

Responsibility for information technology within tourist boards often resides within a finance and administration department, reflecting the role of data which, traditionally, has been for administrative purposes-accommodation grading, publications etc. There is a clear need for information technology, as it pertains to marketing, to be managed directly by the marketing function. This should also include the needs of Visitor Services, which often implement their own information technology systems in isolation of overall marketing demands.

In the past destinations, for example states in Australia have created reservation services operated by the public sector itself within tourist board activity. Indeed in the case of Queensland this extended as far as creating their own package tour operation. However, around the world the current political climate is such that activities which can be more effectively handled by the private sector are being moved to it. In the case of tourism this creates a 'handover' issue between the activities of public sector tourism promotion and the sales activity of the private sector.

The handover between public sector and private sector was not an issue in the past because the entire marketing chain from awareness to trip departure probably took several months or even a year. Today the whole process can take a matter of minutes and an effective partnership between the public and private sector needs to be identified. Debate is ongoing about which place in the marketing chain is the most efficient to effect this handover. A trend is now evolving towards private sector organisations, call centre specialists, operating destination marketing systems, contracted by the tourist board to provide information to potential visitors, and also able effectively to sell travel products and services. It is important that these organisations are not seen to compete with travel agents and tour operators, but embrace the industry as a partner.

Destination Marketing Systems and their operators are attractive to the consumer, as they provide 'one-stop shopping'. In contracting out the service a destination can ensure that performance targets for servicing customers, which it may not previously have been able to meet on its own, are adhered to and that, as a result, the consumer receives better service. Contracts will typically consist of payment to the operator, by the destination, for time spent on information calls offset by commission earned on reservation activity. Other options include

— a handover to a private sector reservation service, after the information stage, if the destination already has an existing information call centre it wishes to continue to operate,

— a joint venture operation with the private sector and

— a co-operative venture owned by partners such as associations, and private sector players with complementary interests, such as communications companies, financial services companies etc.

Each of these options has its own attraction to particular destinations but the entire outsourcing is the cleanest, most efficient and easiest to manage.

Positioning

Position is a form of market communication that plays a vital role in enhancing the attractiveness of a tourism destination. The World Travel and Tourism Council claimed that tourism was the world's largest industry in 1991. The past few years have shown a steady increase in the volume of international travel, and along with this growth in travel, the number of tourism destination choices has also increased as many policy-makers have recognized the value of tourism to the economies of their regions. To some extent, this increased travel can also be attributed to an increase in advertising, as tourism marketers try to enlarge their share of the global tourism pie by promoting their destinations to specific target markets. For example in 1987, Canada and Australia decided to increase advertising in Japan and this resulted in an increase in Japanese visitors of 55% and 33% respectively.

One of the most effective tools in tourism marketing is positioning. The objective of positioning is to create a distinctive place in the minds of potential customers. A position that evokes images of a destination in the customers mind; images that differentiate the destination from the competition and also as a place that can satisfy their needs and wants. Positioning is a communications strategy that is the natural follow-through of market segmentation and target marketing. Since market segmentation is based on the notion that different tourism destinations appeal to different types of tourists, target market segments must be selected before tourism marketers can begin to entice these potential customers. An effective positioning strategy provides a competitive edge to a destination that is trying to convey its attractiveness to the target market.

Positioning is more than just image creation. This important form of market communication helps to distinguish tourism destinations from similar destinations so that customers can choose the one that is the most attractive. Thus, true positioning differentiates a destination from its competitors on attributes that are meaningful to customers and gives it a competitive edge. However, this is a complex process that requires careful analysis of the attributes of destinations and the needs of the target markets. Selection of a positioning strategy that creates a distinctive place in customers' minds is essential in preventing the following pitfalls.

— The destination is forced into a position of competing directly with a stronger competitor. For example, a destination that is further from the source of its visitors may be relegated to a secondary or tertiary level of competition with destinations that are closer to the market.

— The destination's position is so unclear that its target market does not recognize the message that is being sent to them. This often happens when a destination tries to be all things to all people.

— The destination has no identity or has a negative image in customers' minds and does not create customer demand.

According to the basic principles of marketing, products and services are created to solve customer "problems" and provide benefits. Thus, to be effective, positioning must promise the benefit the customer will receive, create the expectation, and it offer a solution to the customer's problem. If at all possible, the solution should be different from and better than the competition's solution set, especially if the competitors are already offering a similar solution.

Positioning should be a single-minded concept, an umbrella from which everything eke in the organization flows. Properly targeted, single-minded positioning affects everything a destination does or stands for, not only advertising, but also all of its promotions. Positioning also affects policies and procedures, employee attitudes, customer relations, complaint handling, and the myriad of other details that combine to make the tourism experience. Tourism services compete on more than just image, differentiation, and benefits offered. There must be a consistency among the various offerings and it is the positioning statement that guides this consistency. Likewise, although positioning can be applied for an entire country, a given area, or a specific city, tourism officials should develop a consistent message if the country plans to use one market to generate business for another. There are two tests of effective positioning. First, the position must be believable in the tourist's mind. Second, the destination must deliver that promise on a consistent basis.

One of the biggest challenges faced by tourism marketers is that the product is largely intangible. Some would argue otherwise, because what is more important than the hotel room, the meal, the beach, the ocean, and the mountains? These are all tangible aspects of the tourism destination. However, these tangibles are what is being "sold", but not what is being "marketed". If we were selling beaches or mountains, what difference would it make where the tourist went, assuming a comparable level of quality? 'What we are marketing, of course, are intangibles. The tangibles are essential and necessary but as soon as they reach a certain level of acceptance, they become secondary. Because they are so difficult to differentiate, to be competitive, the intangibles have to be marketed. Even as tangibles, mountains and beaches have a measure of intangibility because they are experienced rather than possessed.

If tourism products are mostly intangible, they have to be marketed with tangible evidence. This is what is referred to as "tangibilizing the intangible." However, this is a complicated process. By emphasizing the concrete elements one may fail to differentiate oneself from the competition, and since the intangible elements are abstract, by emphasizing the abstract one compounds the intangibility. Thus, tourism destination positioning should foçus on enhancing and differentiating abstract realities by manipulating the tangible clues.

Unfortunately, being aware of this need does not ease the problem. It is still difficult to find meaningful tangible evidence that supports intangible constructs. What must be done, is to create a "position" in the tourist's mind. That is why positioning relies heavily on target marketing. The mental constructs held by the target market must be known, as well as the tangible evidence that sustains them. Positioning, then, is a relative term. It is not simply how the destination is perceived, but how the perceived image performs in relation to competing images. It is the customer's mental perception which may, or may not, differ from the actual physical characteristics. It is most important when, the product is an intangible and there is little difference among the competition regarding the physical characteristics.

The positioning process consists of the various steps needed to develop an effective positioning strategy. This process must be continuous to keep up with changes in the environment including the changing needs of the customer and the competitors tactics. Developing a positioning strategy for a destination in the United States to attract visitors from Japan will be used as a test case to illustrate the steps in the positioning process.

Market Positioning

Market positioning is the first step and is defined as the

process of identifying and selecting markets or segments that represent business potential, to determine the criteria for competitive success. This must be based on a thorough knowledge of the needs, wants, and perceptions of the target market, along with the benefits offered by the destination. The reality of the matter is that if the target market doesn't perceive the image, the image does not exist. If the target market does not believe that what the destination has to offer is a benefit, it isn't a benefit. If the target market doesn't believe that the benefit can be delivered, promises are meaningless. If the benefit isn't important to the target market, it isn't important. If the benefit is not perceived as being different from that of the competition, then differentiation has not succeeded. In short, images, benefits, and differentiation are solely the perception of the tourist, not the perceptions of tourism officials or the tourism marketer.

According to the former United States Travel and Tourism Administration, 3.2 million Japanese inbound travelers, who present a solid market for tourism destinations in the United States, generated $ 10.1 billion in tourism revenue for the U.S. in 1990. The following shows the top ten ranked activities identified by Japanese visitors:

— Sightseeing in cities
— Shopping
— Dining out
— Guided tours
— Visiting landmarks
— Taking pictures
— Beach activities
— Visiting theme parks
— Swimming
— Visiting galleries.

The three highest ranked activities (Sightseeing in Cities, Shopping, and Dining out in Restaurants) seem to provide an advantage to reasonably large cities where these are readily available. In addition, according to Bailey, Japanese persons who are planning to travel to the U.S., initially, do not have a specific destination to visit. Instead, they search for a trip that has several attributes similar to those listed below:

— Some place where other people went

— Reasonable price.

— As many places as possible to cover.

— Minimum contact with local community.

— Perfect Japanese-like service.

— Good food.

— Absolutely free.

Combining these attributes with the top 10 activities listed above, one can an indication of the needs of Japanese visitors. During the trip they like to go to places that have been previously visited by Japanese visitors and where they have opportunities for sightseeing, shopping, and dining. They are very concerned about personal safety, not interested in associating with the local community, and like to receive Japanese-style services. Market positioning research also requires an evaluation of the image that customers have of a tourism destination. This can be used to identify the vital elements which comprise the benefits.

The beauty of a destination, the architecture of a palace, and the historic artifacts in a museum are examples of attributes that may produce a benefit, or may be a tangible representation of an intangible benefit, but are not themselves the benefit. The benefit itself is what the attributes do for the visitor, for instance, a sensation of grandeur, an aura of prestige, or the gaining of knowledge. The credibility of these benefits may diminish rapidly if expectations are not fulfilled. Architecture is soon forgotten if the tour bus breaks down on the return trip. The impression of grandeur loses credibility if visitors feel that their personal safety is threatened. It is the fulfillment of expectations or the inability to, that creates the perception of deliverability for the tourist.

Benefits, like positioning, exist in the mind of the customer and are determined only by asking the customer. Only after this information is obtained, can a destination match its strengths to the visitors' needs and the benefits sought. This knowledge will also provide a basis for the development of a credible differentiation strategy.

Psychological Positioning

Psychological positioning is a strategy employed to create a unique product image with the objective of creating interest and attracting visitors. Since it exists solely in the mind of the visitor, it can occur automatically without any effort on the part of the marketer and any kind of positioning may result. Two very dissimilar destinations may be perceived as the same; two similar destinations may be perceived as different. What the marketer hopes to do is to control the positioning, not just let it happen. Moreover, failure to select a position in the marketplace, to achieve, and to hold that position may lead to various consequences, all undesirable, as pointed out earlier. There are two kinds of psychological positioning in marketing: objective positioning and subjective positioning. Each has its appropriate place and usage.

Objective Positioning

Objective positioning is concerned, almost entirely, with the objective attributes of the physical product. It means creating an image about the destination that reflects its physical characteristics and functional features. It is usually concerned with what actually is, what exists. For example,

Colorado is mountainous and the French Quarter is in New Orleans. However, objective positioning need not always be concrete. It may be more abstract than these examples. The French Quarter is in New Orleans which is also "the birthplace of jazz."

Objective positioning can be very important and is often used in the tourism industry. If a destination has some unique feature, that feature may be used to objectively position the destination, to create an image, and to differentiate it from the competition. If objective positioning is to be used to position the U.S. among Japanese visitors or tour operators any of the unique scenic landmarks, such as the Grand Canyon or Niagara Falls, could be used to show the size and magnitude of these attractions. However, this needs to be linked with other attributes and expectations of the Japanese visitor including "seeing as many places as possible,"; and especially, "where others have been before."

Less successful objective positioning occurs when the feature is not unique. This is why many destination promotions with pictures of beaches fail to create a distinct image or successfully differentiate the product. Other unsuccessful approaches may include a picture of two people looking at a mountain that looks like any other mountain or lying on a beach that looks like any other beach. One of the first rules of effective positioning is uniqueness.

Subjective Positioning

Subjective positioning is concerned with subjective attributes of the destination. Subjective positioning is the image, not of the physical aspects of the destination, but other attributes perceived by the tourist. These perceptions and the resulting images may not necessarily reflect the true state of the destination's physical characteristics. They may simply exist in the tourist's mind and not all tourists' imaging agree with a particular perception or image. Using the previous example of the Grand Canyon or Niagara Falls, subjective positioning would emphasize the awe-inspiring feelings experienced at these natural attractions rather than their physical attributes. Thus, a visit to the Grand Canyon becomes a far greater experience than viewing the physical land formation. What the marketer hopes is that the people in the target market will agree on a favorable image whether or not the image is true. This is the test of effective subjective positioning.

Positioning Approaches

This is the final step in the positioning process, and there are several different approaches to positioning any tourism destination. 'While psychological positioning creates an image, this positioning approach completes the picture, using visual and words, to reinforce what the destination does best and what benefits are offered. Tourism marketers may decide to select the most appropriate of the following approaches, depending on the information gathered during market and psychological positioning. Positioning by attribute, feature, or customer benefit. For this strategy, emphasis is placed on the benefits of the particular features or attributes of the destination. For example, Thailand promotes the friendliness of its people with the statement "The world meets in the land of smiles."

Price Based Positioning

International destinations are not usually positioned on the basis of price because lower prices may be perceived as connoting lower quality. However, value offered to visitors can be effectively utilized as exemplified by Malaysia which claims "Malaysia gives more natural value." With this positioning statement Malaysia is appealing not only to the sense of value but also to its natural attractions.

Positioning with respect to use or application: Here a destination is positioned based on the reasons for visiting it. Bermuda positions itself to the American meetings market with "Sometimes you have to leave the country to get any work done" which promises productive meetings in a relaxed environment. Cancun, Mexico is positioned as "The meeting place for sun worshipers."

Positioning according to the users or class of users: In this case, positioning features the people who should visit the destination. Hong Kong appeals to the incentive travel market with the statement 'When they've reached the top, send them to the peak," referring to Victoria Peak, a major tourist site in Hong Kong: Fisher Island, a luxury residential development in Florida, positions itself as the place "where people who run things can stop running."

Positioning with respect to a product class: This technique is often used to associate a destination with experiences that are extraordinary and/or unique. For example, the Principality of Monaco is positioned as "The fairy tale that does not end at midnight," or holding a convention in Thailand is "Smooth as silk where the sky's the limit, or "If your looking for an ideal meeting place, here's one that's close to heaven" for Israel.

Positioning vis-a-vis the competition: This approach is used when it is necessary to meet the competition head-on; to bring out differences between destinations. This approach is not used frequently in international tourism destination marketing since it may involve negative statements about another country or region. However, it is regularly employed in product and services marketing. For example, Visa credit cards compete with American Express by showing examples of places from around the world that do not accept American Express and only Visa cards are accepted. Ritz-Carlton Hotels is a little more subtle when they say, 'After a day of competition, you deserve a hotel that has none."

Any of these approaches could be used to position the U.S. the minds of Japanese visitors. For example, since Japanese visitors want to go where other Japanese tourists have already been, positioning according to users or a class of users may be appropriate. By developing a creative campaign, an operator can market the fact that many Japanese visitors have been to the Grand Canyon, and were impressed by its awe-inspiring presence. This may include testimonials from previous visitors or tour operators who can make a direct appeal to the target market. However, since the feeling of awe is an intangible construct, positioning statements must show a tangible example to illustrate this feeling. Positioning is the ultimate weapon in niche marketing.

Development of Destination Databases

Destination database development not only responds to marketing needs in the "Age of the Individual" but focuses directly on the question of who will control information flow and market access within the tourism industry. The Computer Reservation System (CRS) environment is remaining unsettled as the mega CRS's go through a consolidation period. These large systems are increasingly seeking to expand their coverage on non-airline travel services such as hotels, car rentals, etc. As the use of technology grows, so does the appreciation of personal service. The younger generation is computer literate and will take greater advantage of travel industry computer applications in making travel decisions.

More reservations will be made from home or from the office especially in regard to domestic travel. A larger slice of the budget of travel organizations will be allocated to direct marketing through computerized database applications. Marketing effectiveness will be measured by visitor arrivals or room nights won, not ad impressions counted. Each of these trends has an application for tourism marketing and argues for the development of destination database capability.

Objectives

The individual tourist product supplier has some fairly straightforward expectations in respect to database activity. He wants it to assist him:

— To know more about what his existing and potential customers want.

— To reach these customers and tell them what he has.

— To satisfy his customers so that they come back and spread the good word.

— To operate profitably.

For the government sector the objectives will be more complex in view of its broader range of responsibilities. The specifics of what it would be seeking from a destination database / management program would be determined by its strategic direction and plans. In broad terms, however, it will be looking for an enhanced program to assist it to:

— Foster an environment in which tourism can grow.

— Contribute more to that growth through well directed marketing, training, information services, and, where appropriate, regulation.

— Distribute tourism growth to better utilize available capacity and preserve environmental resources, and meet economic development objectives. As economists, ERA feels this last factor is particularly important. More and more destinations realize it is not the number of tourists that count but getting the tourists that provide the most positive economic impact.

— Maximize net economic and social benefit from tourism development.

For the consumer, the objectives are to simplify and speed up the travel decision process. They look for a system that will help them to:

— Make individual choices from a broad menu of travel and activity options.
— Receive timely and accurate destination and travel information.
— Simplify access into the travel information labyrinth.
— Resolve concerns and confirm expectations.
— Save (or make) money.

Database Marketing Support Program

A database marketing support program that responds to the trends and contributes to the achievement of the objectives will consist of three main elements:

— The product database.
— The customer database.
— The booking and reservation system to tie them all together.

Product database

Many destinations have or are developing a computerized product database. This is an important asset. The product inventory system provides:

1) descriptive and timely information on many facilities, attractions, accommodations, services, special events, and programs;

2) phone numbers and contacts for use by consumers, agents and other travel intermediaries, thus facilitating the marketing and utilization of the industry products and services;

3) a fulfillment program retrieves information from the database and generates names and address from

consumer inquiries. Of particular significance, perhaps, is this ability to capture customer data. This provides the foundation for expansion into a wide range of customer database marketing.

Possibly the most important consideration is that the product database has the flexibility and other attributes needed for computerized reservations. The CRS cannot deliver its benefits without a complete, well structured, and flexible product database. This is a time for a destination to be proactive in the control and presentation of its inventory. If not, the prospect is there for others to spot the opportunity and establish their own links with the tourist operators.

Customer database

An increase in targeted marketing requires an increase in customer data. In the future, those who have not taken advantage of what computer technology can offer to reach individual consumers, will be at a competitive disadvantage. The consumers are

1. The Visitors Themselves
   - Those on existing databases and those added when they contact a tourism organization.
   - Past visitors on whom data can be obtained.
   - Non-visitors whose travel habits and characteristics indicate they could be future visitors.
2. Those That Influence The Visitors
   - Travel agents and tour operators. The ATC's Tourtrax database is an excellent example of this for North America.
   - Association meeting planners, clubs, corporations, and specialized tour operators.
   - Transportation suppliers including airlines, train operators, cruise lines and automobile associations.

— Hotel chains, car rental companies and other travel industry services.

Structure of database

The structure of a customer database serves two principal functions: 1) to understand existing visitors and 2) to gather information to encourage repeat visitors and reach new visitors.

In understanding existing visitors, certain traditional visitor information is provided for in the customer record. This includes customer demographics, travel patterns and activity profile, expenditure data, triggering cues and information sources, past trip evaluation and satisfaction, and transaction history. This record is kept current and accurate through frequent updating and customer contact. This traditional information is valuable but only the first step in using customer databases. What is also needed is information to reach new visitors through database technology. Here, database technology can be used to address each of four priorities of market circumstance:

1. *Existing Market Segments*: This comprises existing visitors. Concentrating on these segments is the first priority because these are the types of customers who have already expressed the highest interest in our destination by their purchase behavior. Other members of these segments are more likely to visit than members of other segments.
2. *Proximate Potential Market Segments*: These include visitors to nearby destinations with similar characteristics. These customers have indicated the purchase similar products to what we offer. It is not necessary to persuade them to visit an unknown destination, but only to travel to our destination.
3. *Expanded Potential Market Segments*: This comprises travelers who seek similar products to what we offer but

do not now visit the region. They do not need to be persuaded to seek new satisfactions but to satisfy them in our region and destination.

4. *Potential Market Segments for Additional/Enhanced Products*: These market segments are potential visitors if additional or enhanced products are offered. These might be a new type of resort, convention/conference facilities, opening of new recreation resources, or infrastructure improvements. These segments need to be convinced to try out new products we are not known for.

To reach these potential new customers, we need to look at databases that identify customers like our existing visitors, people who visit nearby areas, and visitors who are looking for products we might want to develop. To find people like our existing visitors, we need to gather information about existing visitors that leads us to databases of persons with similar characteristics. For example, we need to get information on their product ownership and brand loyalties, affinity group and club membership, readership patterns, business and occupation profile, etc. This information allows is to identify likely databases that will contain new, high prospect customers

Customer Database Development

There is no easy way for a tourism body to create a comprehensive database of its visitors. Visitors use a wide range of travel services through which customer information can be obtained. There are, nevertheless, a number of steps that can be taken to extend the customer database. The first and most vital step is to develop and maintain a product database and take advantage of the customer inquiry/reservation information it develops. Other steps include:

— Systematically gather information from those visiting tourism visitor centers, parks and other publicly owned attractions and facilities.

— Reach information-sharing agreements with other tourism related land and facility management groups (e.g., airports) to share visitor data.

— Collect data from those who telephone or send in coupons from Tourism advertising.

— Extend and regularly update data on the select list of travel agents and tour operators. Maintain a well structured coverage of associations, special interest clubs and corporations, especially with respect to convention and incentive travel.

— Share information on visitors with the air and cruise lines, the hotel chains and car rental companies and take advantage of opportunities to share information on visitors.

— Develop customer data in the course of research surveys. This is not the traditional demographic and travel patterns information, but information that will help you reach future customers through database technology.

— Be alert for opportunities to purchase outside databases that correspond to known customer characteristics—e.g., brand loyalty, product ownership, media habits, activity participation, and memberships.

An expanded customer database and improved computer capability provide the best opportunities for additional marketing applications directly to individuals.

Following are some uses of destination database marketing

1. *Marketing Planning*: Information is the basis of planning. With it you can target marketing to maximum effect. Without it, you guess or aim and hope. The product and

customer databases are core elements of an information management program. They tell you what you have and who may want to buy it. They provide marketing direction and the ability to monitor effectiveness.

2. *Telemarketing*: A comprehensive and accessible product database empowers staff to not just provide information but also to direct customer interest and to sell. They can highlight the strong points of a hotel or resort and convey their own local knowledge and enthusiasm. Giving callers something that makes them feel they are getting inside knowledge is a powerful selling tool.
3. *Repeat Customer Development*: Destinations should favorably consider the establishment of a loose but structured association with its repeat visitors. As frequent flyer clubs, hotel clubs, and the like have shown, such an association can offer a number of marketing opportunities. Clubs generate a sense of loyalty in many of their members. At the same time, they act as a defense against others who may be trying to persuade your visitors to go elsewhere.

The benefits of membership can be as simple as a membership certificate and a club newsletter giving advance information on new attractions, prices and events. With the cooperation of the private sector, they can go all the way to price discounts, preferred reservations, etc. One example of such a destination area club is "Club France." This is considered by the French Government Tourist Office to be a great marketing asset. It is now at the stage where, with the help of the private sector, the benefits are substantial and the members are prepared to pay $65 per year for the privilege of belonging.

4. *Relational Database Marketing Applications*: The prime purpose of such applications is to link the customer information in your database with databases that allow you to reach more customers. What is involved is the comparison of your database with others that share the

same characteristics as your visitors. Relational database work is one of the most productive ways to expand the breadth of your own customer database. You may find new groups of people (and individuals) you had not even tried to reach in the past but that are now revealed as good prospects.

Computer Reservation System (CRS)

The CRS is changing the way we do things, changing the structure of the travel industry and causing travel marketing to be irrevocably changed. It is the means of market access. Everyone in the travel business has to face up to it. Sitting on the sidelines and doing nothing is hardly an option anymore. Those who do that will be left behind. Any one seeking growth cannot afford to be disconnected from his markets by this technology. Action has to be taken to protect customers in an environment in which there are others with the technology base to take them away.

Destinations and individual or chain facilities looking at the CRS options should remember that the airlines often regard other bookings and providing travel information as an ancillary service. Sabre and Covia's Apollo each currently have about 20,000 hotels worldwide listed in their systems. The hotels listed, however, are mainly those of the major chains plus independent properties that are particularly well know. These systems also contains basic data on destinations such as the weather, perhaps a map and some of the principal attractions. The big tourist destinations receive most of the attention. These are the ones that will be most often requested and that will, therefore, be the most viable in terms of income to the CRS and cost to the organization being listed.

Although there will be more non-airline activity in these CRS's, it seems unlikely that this will involve the thousands of small hotels, attractions, and special interest operations that are scattered throughout a country or region. The volume of requests that one of these would receive would be too small to make this worthwhile. Also, the mega CRS's are too preoccupied with other priorities to handle such listings. They are busy on research and development and on vying with one another for dominance.

Airline CRS

When talking of linkage, the emphasis is not on the question of the storage of the destination's full product in the airline CRS but on enabling that CRS to draw on the product the destination has to offer, when the situation arises. A link with an airline CRS does not rule out the continuance of the destination CRS. On the contrary, the benefits a destination receives from its own CRS will still be there. The service provided by the airline CRS in reaching markets is an added element not a replacement. There are a number of "universal interfaces" that have been or are being developed. They can act as the link between a destination specific CRS and a variety of airline CRS's. Entering into this kind of linkage is less a case of, "if" than of "when".

So what should be done? No individual destination has the budget to compete in the mega CRS battle. The airline CRS's cannot deliver to most of the individual properties and attractions in a destination on a cost justifiable basis and are not currently very interested in doing so. Some action needs to be taken nevertheless. What is needed is a destination based CRS that for the time being operates independently.

The overall goal is to increase the volume and value of tourism to and within the destination. A destination database with CRS capability can serve this goal in the following ways.

— It provides improved market access for the full range of tourism enterprises—the inns, the small fishing operator, the craft shop, etc. No other system will give them center stage and the marketing thrust that it implies.

— A destination CRS would be available through a toll free telephone and fax number to access the market that does not book through travel agents.

— A destination CRS places the destination in control. Demand can be directed so as to maximize the utilization of capacity or to serve other purposes. The CRS is the medium through which the destination can operate a strong telemarketing program.

— It is also the most fruitful source of expanding the destination's customer database. This provides a great opportunity to find out more about the inquirers and their interests.

— Leading on from that is the ability the system offers for the development of accurate and up-to-date statistical data. It makes possible more detailed market performance analysis and evaluation of advertising effectiveness.

— The destination CRS will make it easier for both travel agents and individuals to make bookings. Speed is an increasingly important consideration in making a travel decision and confirmation.

— A destination CRS will assist the development of closer cooperation between the public and private sectors.

— The reservations system will greatly assist in making maximum use of the investment made in development of the product and customer databases.

— The customer database can be made available to provide a list of customers to the private sector for direct marketing. Imagine, the tourism organization demonstrates its worth by actually providing a list of customers— rather than attempting to justify a marketing budget based on measures of advertising recall.

Destination Web Strategy in Hospitality

Many destinations have suffered steep declines in visitors over the past three years. And while travel to some destinations is down by 10%, 15% and in some cases 20%, online travel to these same destinations has grown by 30% annually over the past three years. Hoteliers cannot control the amount of travel to their destinations. At the same time Internet-savvy hoteliers can dramatically increase their online market share at the expense of their competitors that are "asleep at the wheel". Hoteliers that employ robust Destination Web Strategies have an effective means to capture new lucrative markets, boost direct distribution and decrease the need for intermediaries.

A Destination Web Strategy means leveraging the popularity of your destination to your own advantage by making your hotel or cluster of hotels the "hero" of the destination, and in the same time turning your hotel website into a valuable destination resource for your online customers and increasing its value and relevance for the search engines. This strategy is one of the most effective means to market a local property or a cluster of properties within a particular destination. It allows the hotel to leverage the richness of the destination and shape the local attributes of its environment with creative marketing initiatives that appeal to its online customer base. The strategy is also an imperative for hoteliers to highlight the property within the context of local resources, because local government sponsored initiatives to promote the richness of the destination, which includes your hotel, are quickly diminishing.

Hotel planning is destination sensitive. When searching for accommodations on the Internet, consumers usually use keywords based on the name of the destination +hotel, e.g. "Boston Hotel". An estimated 85% of Internet users rely on search engines to locate information on the

Web. Independent hotels, branded hotels, hotel management companies and lodging companies must all rely on search engine referrals. So by having a robust Destination Web Strategy, the search engines will be able to find additional value in your website, catalog and index the website more effectively, associate it more specifically with various local attractions, lifestyle attributes and aspects of the destination, and drive more business to the property.

Hoteliers able to leverage the popularity of their destination, matched with a well-defined hotel product mix, can capture more online market share and boost conversion rates. The key ingredient is by promoting the many facets of the hotel and cluster of hotels and its relationship to the destination. This approach allows for creative flexibility by making the hotel always the center of attention, the "hero of the destination."

Types of Destination Web Strategy

A Destination Web Strategy can take many forms and shapes based on the particular destination or business environment. Here are the most common types of initiatives we at Hospitality eBusiness Strategies have developed for many of our clients:

— *Destination Section or Page*: An optimized destination section or page within the hotel website of a single hotel property or a corporate website that represents a cluster of hotels in a given destination.

— *Destination 1-Pager*: A stand-alone fully optimized one-page website representing a cluster of hotels within a destination.

— *Destination Website (single property)*: A stand-alone website encompassing destination attributes matched with attributes of the hotel. (e.g. eco travelers, gamblers, spa enthusiasts)

— *Destination Web Portal*: A stand-alone multi-page fully optimized website representing a cluster of hotels with local area content, pages targeting different audiences.

Some hotel companies, guided by Internet-savvy consultancies, have already begun employing Destination Web Strategies to counter the disastrous effects of merchant model discounts and better market their product and local destination attributes. Whether the hotelier has one hotel or cluster of hotels, a Destination Web Strategy enables the hotelier to offer a rich, deep, destination focused website with the creative flexibility of appealing to a variety of patrons. These may be: conventions, meetings, groups, business and leisure travelers, lifestyle activity seekers, family, weddings, honeymoons, recreation, etc.

A Destination Web Strategy is an exercise in evaluating the attributes of the destination, the various aspects of the hotel product, and the relevant lifestyle attributes of your existing and potential customers, and packaging it in a presentable manner for the online consumer. The final product becomes a well defined destination-oriented website that serves as the foundation for creative and innovative online marketing and distribution.

You will now be able throw marketing muscle behind various initiatives in response to societal trends, current events, and general shifts in the market place. This strategy is "natural" for the hospitality vertical as the product, by definition, is destination specific.

This strategy involves conceptualizing, developing and optimizing the hotel website to achieve two main goals:

— Provide valuable and relevant destination information so that the online travelers and the search engine spiders alike find value on the website beyond the mere hotel product content

— Turn the hotel into the "gravitational center of the destination"

Developing the Destination Web Strategy is a complex task and requires a combination of Internet, hospitality and destination-specific knowledge and extensive research. Some required steps include:

— Identifying the most popular area attractions

— Identifying the relevant lifestyle categories, attitudes and values of your existing and potential customer base

— Identifying local events that can be exploited to attract guests at the property

— Identifying how local attractions and lifestyle attributes relate to the property

— Identifying patterns of consumer online purchasing habits for the hotel/resort and the particular destination

— Evaluating the most popular target keywords for the destination

— Ranking the keywords according to their popularity and relevance

— Developing credible and relevant copy based on detailed destination research

— Weaving the target keywords throughout the copy

— Developing the "invisible copy": page titles, description tags and meta tags.

— Overhauling your website to add the identified destination, lifestyle and property attributes and position your hotel product as the central point of the destination

The process for building a destination strategy begins by evaluating typology, attributes, and resources in the local environment. Identify your type of destination. Is this an urban destination, suburban destination, ocean or resort destination, mountain destination and so on? Next identify all the external attributes within your area. The destination may offer outdoor recreation services, an extensive transportation infrastructure, seasonal events and attractions, major business districts, conference centers and much more. Finally, based on typology and attributes, what are those particular resources that people need or may desire at the destination? These may include water-based recreation, historical artifacts, cultural resources, dining resources, and business/commerce resources, and many others.

After the destination is analyzed, begin evaluating and introducing the hotel product and the lifestyle attributes of your customer base into the mix. The product mix may include: wedding facility, conference room, meetings and reception area, and concierge services, while the customer profile may include business travelers, senior travelers, and even families with pets.

The lifestyle attributes are more complex. Identifying the attitudes and values of a person or group, and sometimes of people that you have never seen or heard from is inevitably more difficult. It is a matter of perspective on what is truly important to the customer. Different characteristics of the property or destination can appeal to different customer segments. For example, to the business traveler, choosing a hotel may be influenced by the availability of a function room, high-speed Internet access or proximity to an area corporation, while a leisure traveler may find the same hotel a great location for local area attractions; same hotel, same destination, different purpose.

Benefits

The Destination Web Strategy allows for a highly informative, content rich website that encourages site references for increased link popularity that boosts search engine positioning. The creative flexibility of this strategy captures key customer segments and shapes the property with a variety of new, varied and exciting insights for the online consumer. It attracts new customers seeking choice, particular in lifestyle categories, plan meetings or weddings, or provide close proximity to a convention center. This strategy can be configured to appeal to any audience where there is relevance to the local destination.

Since the Internet provides unprecedented flexibility to shape locally relevant content at relatively low cost, a Destination Web Strategy becomes a source of "permanent innovation" for the hotelier. Exploiting the existing popularity of the destination and leveraging the appeal of the local market to various customer segments boosts direct-to-consumer distribution over the Internet at a very reasonable cost. The need is very real as the environment is increasingly more competitive and traditional marketing channels and even government supported efforts are diminishing.

The Destination Web Strategy:

— Allows the hotel brand, hotel management company, branded or independent hotel and resort to leverage the popularity of the destination for the benefit of its property or cluster of properties within a destination

— Allows hoteliers with cluster of properties within the destination to cross-sell their properties and leverage differences in location and price to appeal to a range of travel planning budgets, tastes, and perceived values

— Reduces the overall marketing cost (creation, development, maintenance, and search engine submissions) as the strategy bundles together more than one property, or a single property with the attributes of the destination

— Allows customers to locate a property or group of properties unique to a particular attribute of the destination or a lifestyle category

From an online marketing and distribution standpoint the strategy increases a site's link popularity, boosts positioning on the search engines, creates numerous co-marketing opportunities, expands and lowers cost of pay-per-click marketing, increases the relevancy of targeted email marketing strategies, offers real-time city-wide availability for cross-selling and up-selling, and most importantly creates numerous points of entry online to the property. It's your chance to make your property the champion of the destination!

6

Nature and Types of Hospitality Marketing

The hospitality industry involves service marketing because an intangible product is sold to the ultimate consumer. It is true that guests are in direct contact with tangible products as they stay in a room, watch the television, and use the courtesy products provided for them. However, they are not purchasing those products for later use. The intangible "product" that they are really purchasing is the comfortable feeling of the warm, safe, clean room as well as the individual attention given to each guest by the hotel staff. In the restaurant industry it is often put this way: "Sell the sizzle, not the steak." It is usually not just the meal that brings customers back, but the people who present it. Service marketing frequently gets only one chance to make a good first impression.

The hospitality industry must maintain high standards to meet the expectations of consumers and ensure repeat business. Competition is brisk among the different types of lodging establishments. Whatever the type of hotel, the services offered, or the price range, there is another one like it nearby perfectly willing to try a little harder to earn the customer's dollar. Hotel managers are keenly aware of this fundamental economic principle, and pay close attention to service, customer preferences, and staff training.

Technology has found its way into hotel amenities, those services or items offered to guests for convenience and comfort. With the addition of cable television and movies-on-demand, full-size desks, two-line phones, and modem hook-ups at most hotels, many guest rooms have become "branch offices" for the convenience of the highly profitable business traveler. Some hotels believe that an upscale image and impressive extras gain the loyalty of guests-especially in the higher price ranges. Although luxury amenities cost hotels more, they also attract customers willing to pay the added price.

Importance of Hospitality Marketing

Influence of Finance

Hospitality marketing is part of a larger industry known as travel and tourism. According to the Travel Industry Association of America (TIA), travel and tourism is the largest services export industry in the nation. In fact, in 29 of the 50 states, travel and tourism is either the first, second, or third largest employer. TIA estimated that more than $582 billion was spent in the travel and tourism industry in 1999. That figure translates to 18 million jobs for Americans. About 7.7 million jobs were directly related to travel and tourism, and 10.3 million employees were indirectly related. As a result of those jobs, $159 billion in payroll income was generated. That's billion, not million.

In the hospitality marketing sector, travelers spent over $50 billion on rooms in lodging establishments in 1999 and more than $23 billion on food while traveling. When you add in shopping, entertainment, and miscellaneous items, travelers dropped a total of more than $235 billion into the accounts of the hotel industry. You may not be a typical business traveler making about ten trips a year, but chances are you will probably eat out sometime this week. More than four out of ten people ate at a restaurant on a typical day in 1999. In 1999, 11.3 million people worked in some type of restaurant, making the restaurant industry the nation's largest private-sector employer.

Travel and tourism is good for the economy. Not only do people in the United States travel within the States, called domestic travel, but many international travelers come to America and consequently spend money. United States' travelers spent $81.4 billion while traveling in foreign countries, but international travelers spent more money in America than Americans spent abroad, resulting in a travel trade surplus of $14.2 billion. With the advent of Internetbased travel services such as Priceline and Travelocity, many travelers are organizing and booking their own travel arrangements. Deregulation of the airline industry often translates to lower airline ticket prices. Because travel agents can no longer depend on ticket sales commissions to support their business, they seek to increase revenue by booking other types of trips such as cruises, motor coach travel, or escorted tours.

Travel has a universal appeal to all ages, and several trends are emerging. An aging Baby-Boomer generation has begun to travel often and book tours. People take their children or grandchildren on trips more often. Young people travel more extensively, often as part of a growing number of families who take shorter, but more expensive, vacations. Business travelers bring their families along and combine business with pleasure. The business traveler is no longer predominantly male. Female executives make up almost half the executive traveler market.

Travel and tourism is truly beneficial for the economy. During 1999, domestic and international travelers in the United States spent an average of $1.42 billion a day. If that figure seems hard to comprehend, consider it this way: $1.42 billion a day equals $59.4 million an hour, $989,300 a minute, and $16,400 per second.

Nature

Hotel employees are responsible for providing a comfortable and enjoyable stay for their customers. Lodging facilities operate 24 hours a day, seven days a week. Large hotels may employ hundreds of people to see to the needs of customers or to maintain efficiency in running the establishment.

Management

There are many management positions in a hotel.

— General managers have the responsibility of overseeing the operations of the hotel.

— Front office managers coordinate reservations and room assignments and manage the front desk staff.

— Executive housekeepers supervise the work of the housekeeping staff to ensure guest rooms, meeting rooms, and public areas are clean and inviting.

— Food and beverage managers oversee all activities involved in planning, preparing, and providing meals and drinks for hotel guests in the hotel's restaurants, banquet or meeting areas, and lounges.

— Sales directors supervise the sales staff who may handle corporate accounts, social or special events, conventions and conferences, and exhibits.

— Human resource managers not only deal with recruiting and hiring the hotel staff, but are responsible for training and coordinating employee benefits as well.

— Operations managers keep the hotel running, literally. They take care of security, heating and air conditioning, electrical and power systems, groundskeeping, safety, and maintenance.

— Financial managers supervise procedures involved in tracking a hotel's receipts and expenditures and daily audits.

— Keep in mind that entry-level jobs exist in all of the areas listed above as well as management positions.

A typical hotel or restaurant has two divisions: the front of the house and the back of the house. The front of the house involves any area of the hotel to which the general public or a hotel guest has access. That would include guest rooms, meeting rooms, business center, public restrooms, gift shop, pool, and restaurants on the property. The back of the house includes those vital departments not usually seen or frequented by a guest or patron. Those departments include areas such as human resources, management, accounting, reservations, operations, housekeeping, and banquet operations.

Hotels and Motels

Full-Service Hotels

Hotels are multistoried lodging facilities that range in size from a limited number of rooms to hundreds of rooms. Quality of hotels varies widely with price, location, and age. A full-service hotel provides a wide range of services, usually including a restaurant and bar on the premises, retail shops, luggage assistance, parking lot attendants, room service, and other amenities such as dry cleaning. Business travelers and convention attendees make up the largest percentage of hotel guests.

The growth and lower rates of limited-service hotels have challenged full-service hotels to offer attractive extras to guests. Many hotels offer suites packed with exercise equipment and other trendy items, such as calming fountains and massage chairs. Fitful sleepers can get earplugs or sound boxes that simulate heartbeats, blackout drapes, or even the BioBrite Sunrise Clock, a device that brightens slowly to simulate sunrise. Highquality, brand-name supplies and amenities, from mattresses and mattress covers to designer soaps and lotions, have become standard.

Many hotels offer high-speed Internet access. Marriott International has about 300 hotels worldwide wired for high-speed access and plans to have an additional 200 hotels online by the end of 2001. Hilton Hotels, Radisson Hotels, and Choice Hotels also plan high-speed access in rooms.

The Adam's Mark Hotel in Dallas is offering wireless Web access to business guests who use its meeting rooms. The number of business trips including children grew 32 percent between 1997 and 1998, so Holiday Inn started offering kids' suites for $115. The rates for these rooms, furnished with bunk beds, Lego play table, and Nintendo, are slightly lower than normal. Even some luxury hotels offer amenities for children. An increasing number of hotels accept guests with pets. Hotels usually have rules to keep pets and owners controlled. The cheaper the room, the greater the likelihood of paying an additional fee ranging from $5 to $25 a night to cover cleanup costs, or placing a security deposit as a hedge against damages.

Airport Hotels

Hotels located near airports have often had a reputation for dowdiness and poor service. Recently, millions of dollars have been spent on upgrades. Airy, earth-toned rooms priced from $85 a night contain well-stocked mini bars and features such as spas, dataports, and triple-glazed windows to keep out noise. Weekend rooms often run half the cost of city-center hotels. Airport hotels provide handy accommodations for travelers with early morning flights. Consumers can get a night's sleep-and might save even more by avoiding airport parking lots.

University Hotels

Major universities conduct studies to determine whether hotel/convention centers are good for their campuses. Mixed-use hotel and retail conference complexes provide major universities with first-class hotels complete with conference amenities such as bookstores, public atriums, and a diverse range of retail/entertainment shops and restaurants.

The last decade has seen the expansion and affiliation of many major hotel chains. Summerfield Suites Hotels now franchises its concept, as does Hyatt Hotels Corporation. Although franchise operations expand market penetration, they carry a potential risk if individual franchises fail to live up to standards set by parent companies. New ideas in customer service will continue at a breathtaking pace. Marriott is in the process of opening 30 upscale full-service Gourmet Bean coffee outlets right in its hotels. New ideas in food service will go further, as will luxury amenities in rooms. Some hotels have begun to maintain guest "profiles." to customize rooms for individual tastes.

Motels and Motor Inns

Motels are lodging facilities usually found on feeder highways and roads, or along lesser-known routes. Motels are usually one-story structures, with parking in front of or near the room. Most motels do not have restaurants, and the owner provides all services. The term motel comes from "motor hotel." The invention of the automobile helped the hotel industry become a booming business in the 1920s. Landowners along major routes built wooden 10-foot by 10-foot cabins easily accessible to weary travelers who could park their cars in front. Owners soon expanded their operations to 15 or more cabins referred to as tourist courts.

In the 1930s, the Great Depression devastated the lodging industry. Many smaller motels went bankrupt, and the industry did not revive until after World War II. During the war, troops being transported, workers being transferred to various factories, and families reuniting presented opportunities for new hotels built near major military bases and industrial areas. At the end of the war, air travel became available to larger numbers of people. The growing postwar economy saw companies expand with branch and regional offices, and conventions and conferences offered opportunity to the hospitality industry. Vast numbers of business travelers became the most important customers, but people also traveled more for pleasure as they had more disposable income after the war.

Motor inns are the most common lodging facilities found in the United States. Motor inns are usually located near major highways and the interstate highway system, often clustered with other inns. Motor inns range from two to six stories, and usually have a restaurant or bar. Motor inns are becoming hard to distinguish from hotels, offering bellhops, room service, and increasing amenities. Motor inns located near airports are popular for meeting and convention business. Holiday Inn and Comfort Inn are examples of motor inns. The Superior Small Lodging (SSL) Association is an organization that attempts to ensure tourists receive great value and high-quality accommodations at member properties.

Members member properties. Members include small motels, inns, and bed and breakfasts. This organization helps members by associating with Convention and Visitors Bureaus, Chambers of Commerce, and Tourism Destination Organizations. Motels and motor inns have improved their operations, improved their relationships with customers, and become more effective in competing with other hotels and inns.

Limited-Service Properties

Rising full-service hotel rates have caused planners to look for meeting sites and lodging that are easy on the budget. Growing numbers of limited-service properties provide primarily sleeping rooms without expensive amenities such as food service. Extended-stay facilities are limited-service properties offering residential-style units with multi-room plans and kitchen facilities to attract business travelers or those relocating. Summerfield Suites, AmeriSuites, and Residence Inns by Marriott are examples of limited-service, extended-stay properties serving the meeting market. Training that may last weeks is now often booked at limited-service hotels near major airports. Meeting rooms vary from a small bedroom to a room with a 50-person capacity.

Meeting space at limited-service hotels can be as large as 1,250 square feet, and is comparatively inexpensive or may be complimentary. Full-service hotels usually charge between $5 and $10 per square foot for meetings. Limited-service hotels charge flat rates of $50 to $150 for day meetings, frequently including morning and afternoon coffee and soda breaks. Rates go lower when groups book sleeping rooms. Many limited-service properties offer suites with two bedrooms and two bathrooms. Most business travelers do not like to share one-bedroom rooms. Executives, who realize that most business travelers do not like to share rooms, can give trainees their own bedrooms and baths for $20 less per night than at a full-service hotel.

Economy of lodging idustry

The economy segment of the lodging industry faces constant change. Goals for success include a good price/value ratio and guest satisfaction. Added amenities and services result in rising room rates, and the pressure to add amenities is strong. Rates cannot exceed guests' perception of the hotel's value, however, for the business to stay competitive. Major economy hotel chains attempt sophisticated marketing efforts. Consumers remember the "We'll leave the light on for you" tag line that Motel 6 uses. Several chains have automated reservations system interfaces to appeal to travel agents.

The bottom line for economy lodging is to offer a lot for a little. Budget Host has more than 180 inns with 7,300 guest rooms located in 37 states and Canada. Amenities offered by Budget Host include king- and queen-size beds, cable television and movie channels, complimentary coffee, microwaves, refrigerators, free continental breakfast, swimming pool, picnic area, suites, at-door and truck parking, and connecting rooms.

Bed and Breakfasts (B & Bs)

Bed and breakfasts (B & Bs) are lodging facilities that include breakfast in the cost of the room. This concept is common in the United Kingdom and is gaining popularity in the United States. In Europe it is common to rent a room in a single-family household. B & Bs evolved from this concept of renting sleeping rooms in a home with shared common space. Sometimes, bathrooms are shared by several guest rooms. B & Bs began to appear in the United States in the late 1960s. There are now more than 20,000 B & Bs, an increase of 18,000 since 1979. The industry shows an increasing average number of rooms per property, growing occupancy rates, and an increasing number of support services. There are a wide variety of B & B accommodations available.

B & B homestays are private, owner-occupied residences with up to five guest rooms available to visitors. Breakfast is often the only meal served and is included in the charge for the room. B & B inns are commercially licensed businesses operated in a building that primarily provides overnight accommodations though the owner may live on the premises. The number of guest rooms for a B & B inn ranges from a minimum of four to a maximum of 25. Breakfast may be the only meal served, or other meals may be available. Country inns are commercially licensed businesses primarily known for cuisine, usually away from commercial areas. Country inns offer overnight accommodations and a full-service breakfast and dinner to overnight guests and/or the public. The number of guest rooms ranges from a minimum of four to a maximum of 20.

Key to the success of B & Bs is that they offer an experience different from that of other lodging. B & Bs appeal to weary travelers who desire personal service from consistent innkeepers as opposed to an anonymous front desk staff. B & B guests often seek a relaxing, private experience different from stays of most corporate travel. Repeat guests sometimes become part of the innkeeper's life. Successful innkeepers learn about travelers' families, their birthdays, and even their food preferences.

More and more business travelers are seeking out B & Bs as an alternative to the anonymity and sameness of hotels and motels. Corporate guests are sometimes hesitant about staying in an inn, but discover that accommodations are often better than at a hotel and provide the comfort of home. A recent survey of innkeepers and B & B owners indicates that business travelers account for about half of their annual overnight stays. Corporate travelers account for a great portion of repeat business at inns that meet their expectations.

As with other parts of the lodging industry, the key to success is increasing amenities. Private baths are a necessity. Innkeeper Jeff Archuleta, who runs Napoleon's Retreat Bed and Breakfast in St. Louis, says that business travelers won't even consider sharing a bath. Private baths, flexible cancellation policies to accommodate last-minute changes in travel plans, flexible check-in/out times to accommodate flight schedules, private key access so guests can come and go as they please, and policies prohibiting children and pets are key features for attracting business travelers. Other services and amenities desired by business travelers include firm mattresses, desks, private telephones, exercise equipment, dataports, fax machines, and copy machines. Privacy is one of the most important services an innkeeper can offer business guests.

Resorts and Conferemce Centres

Resorts

Resorts are hotels or motels located in popular vacation areas that offer recreational activities related to or in addition to attractions in the area. The resort may provide golf, horseback riding, tennis, skiing, tours, social activities, unique dining, or day trips. Resorts offer deluxe rooms with a wide range of prices. Rooms with a scenic view and more space command higher prices. Dude ranches, ski resorts, casino hotels, and health resorts are examples of specialized resorts. Resorts may be chains or individually owned. Some resorts are open only "in season," but many resorts are open yearround with indoor pools and big-name entertainment. Resorts offer package deals that vary in price at different times of the year.

Warm resort areas cost more from November through March. Ski resorts charge their highest rates during the winter season. The best rates are offered by resorts during offpeak season. Major airlines may work with resorts to offer travelers package deals that include the price of the flight and the hotel. The growing senior population has changed the focus of some resorts. Branson, Missouri has become a popular resort for senior citizens to visit. Places like Phoenix, Arizona and Georgetown, Texas offer attractive accommodations for senior citizens. Bingo, craft classes, light exercise sessions, and other social activities make resorts fun meeting places for seniors. As Baby Boomers age, they too will affect the nature of resort accommodations.

Condominiums (condos), when considered as a part of the lodging industry, are living quarters owned by private persons that are rented out to the public most of the year. Most condos are apartments in high-rise buildings located at beaches or other recreational areas. Owners consider condos to be good investment properties. Timeshares involve buying a specific time period (one or two weeks) to spend at a vacation resort. The price of the timeshare depends on the time of the year chosen. February would be a popular season in a warm resort area such as Cancun, Mexico. Timeshare owners can swap dates or property with other timeshare owners.

Resort and conference-center marketing is a lot more than selling rooms. The central theme is to provide a great guest experience. Guests don't buy a place to stay. They buy the expectation of a great experience. Successful marketers see their property through the eyes of the guests. They try to learn from guests what they really value in a resort or conference center in order to provide great experiences.

Conference Centres

Aconference center is a large meeting venue surrounded by enough hotels to accommodate multiple conventions or conferences simultaneously. Every year, growing cities with good airport hubs discuss the possibility of building convention or conference centers. City leaders realize the revenue potential from a successful conference center. There must be a large number of hotel rooms close to the convention center, efficient public transportation, a wide array of restaurants to accommodate guests, and additional tourist attractions.

The elegant, award-winning Orange County Convention Center in Orlando, Florida will grow to 2.1 million square feet of exhibit space by 2003. This amount of space will accommodate large shows and smaller conferences at the same time. Orlando has plans to add 23,000 additional hotel rooms, increasing the inventory to 99,000 rooms. The prestigious Peabody Orlando will build a 1,000-room, 42-story tower linked to the Convention Center. Universal Orlando will develop hotels, a golf course, and a theme park on 2,000 acres of land.

Transportation, dining, and recreation are important features for a successful conference center. Orlando's

International Airport will accommodate 70 million passengers annually by 2003. Nearly 400 restaurants in Orlando provide conference attendees with numerous dining choices. Outlet malls and an upscale Millennium Mall scheduled to open in 2004 add to Orlando's convention-center amenities.

Cleveland, Ohio may seem a less-likely place for a conference center when compared to Orlando, Florida, but the Cleveland Convention Center advertises 20,000 hotel rooms in the greater Cleveland area with 3,200 rooms downtown. The city has a good array of attractions from professional sports to art museums. Rapidly growing Indianapolis has hotels, restaurants, shopping centers, professional sports, and a major airport to meet the needs of most conventions. Indianapolis and Cleveland may not sound as glamorous as Orlando, but both of these cities have what convention centers need to succeed: accessible locations, transportation, hotel rooms, meeting-room space, and community attractions to accommodate a wide array of conferences.

Restaurants

Competition among restaurants gives consumers endless choices for dining. Thousands of restaurants open and close every year. Some of the restaurants are part of well-recognized chains while others are independent operations. Keys to successful restaurants include good food, appropriate prices, strong marketing, and sound public relations. Dining out has become big business seven days a week. Busy working families find it easier to dine out or have food delivered. Look up restaurants in the yellow pages of the telephone book, and you find a long list of possibilities. No matter what type of restaurant consumers choose, they expect good quality food for the price and excellent customer service.

Dining options range from reasonably priced fast food to expensive meals served at full-service restaurants. Higher prices increase customer expectations for the dining experience. The National Restaurant Association defines three primary types of restaurants. Table service, quick service, and on-site food service make up the organization's membership. Within these larger groups lies an almost endless variety of menus and prices.

Table-service Restaurants

Table-service restaurants, as the name implies, are those that serve customers personally at the table. Beyond that large distinction, there are many types of table-service operations.

Fine dining, or white-tablecloth service, provides the highest levels of personal service and more choice of rare food and beverages in a formal or sophisticated setting. The most exclusive restaurants almost always require reservations (if they can be had at all), and may be noted for a particular chef, a unique location, or a long tradition of fine service. Prices for fine dining are usually high, and consumers expect the best -whether the atmosphere is formal or trendy.

Casual dining offers a less-expensive alternative to fine dining, a friendly atmosphere, and more moderate prices. In the last twenty years, national chains such as T.G.I.Friday's, Applebees, and Chili's have established themselves as national leaders, but smaller chains and local establishments attract customers in similar ways. Informal decor, a casual ambience, and a familiar and appealing menu encourage repeat business. These restaurants become regular stops for many people. Casual dining establishments may lack the exhaustive wine list available at a fine dining restaurant, but many beverages are available at reasonable prices. Although there are less expensive restaurants, casual dining places remain popular by selling the sociable mood as much as their menus.

Theme restaurants are a form of casual dining that have also seen the growth of national chains. Many local theme restaurants exist based on such themes as medieval times, old-fashioned parlors, or perhaps most commonly, sports. National chains have brought the consistency of offerings to theme restaurants as well as a distinct experience. Many casual dining restaurants could easily be considered theme restaurants as well. Ethnic restaurants offer an even more distinct experience, depending upon particular national or regional cuisine to draw diners.

Although ethnic restaurants vary as widely as the cultures they represent, in this area, too, national chains have begun standardizing fare. Don Pablo's markets Mexican flavors to a wide audience, and Olive Garden attempts to convey an authentic Italian sense to its food. Restaurant critics might quibble whether these chains offer genuine ethnic food, but they bring a wider variety of tastes to the American palate than were previously available. Prices for most ethnic restaurants, including the national chains, vary as well, but most fall within the same range as casual dining. With changes in population characteristics, many experts predict growth in this field.

Family restaurants, such as Bob Evans or Denny's, offer even more moderate prices and cater to the entire family. Although casual dining establishments usually accept children, family restaurants depend heavily upon those customers who bring young children with them. Alcohol is usually not sold, and breakfast, lunch, and dinner menus are standard. Many locally owned family restaurants have wonderful reputations. Other types of restaurants exist as well. Cafeterias were a once-popular type of restaurant that still do well in some areas. Buffets offer a similar type of service, sometimes with a single price for each diner. Grills and diners cater to the same customers as family restaurants, competing as well in speed of service with fast-food places. In all cases, categories are not hard and fast and there is considerable overlap, and even room for debate. Is Chi-Chi's a casual place, a theme establishment, or an ethnic restaurant?

Quick-Service Restaurants

Despite the many types of table-service restaurants, quick-service sales dominate the food-service industry. Fast food is the largest market in the world for restaurant food. Fast food, as we know it today, grew out of old traditions of single-serving vendors and increasing industrialization of food-service operations. Rapid serving times, appealing products, and reliable quality control throughout the world account for the success of fast-food operations. Although there are local places and small chains, the famous international corporations rule the industry. McDonald's is the largest restaurant chain in the world, with more than 24,000 restaurants. Next in sales in the fast-food list is Burger King, followed by Pizza Hut, KFC, Wendy's, and Taco Bell. Tricon, Inc., owns Pizza Hut, Taco Bell, and KFC, but its combined sales still are less than McDonald's.

The quick-service industry is fiercely competitive, and battles for the convenience-oriented consumer take many forms. New menu items, special pricing promotions, toys for children, and immense advertising campaigns are techniques the fast-food giants use to compete for the huge market. Almost everyone can recite the slogans or even sing a jingle. Still, as fast-food restaurants approach the saturation point in American society, growth in fast food is declining in the United States. The overseas demand continues to grow.

On-Site Food Service

An often overlooked area of the restaurant industry is on-site food service. On-site food service are those food services in business and industry that include institutional, educational, and corporate food services and may include hotel restaurants as well. Although these are not usually thought of as part of the hospitality industry, many of the same principles for planning and operation apply.

Tourism

Tourism is big business for most states, and sizable amounts of money are spent on advertising campaigns to increase tourism. States pay large sums of money to produce creative promotions aimed at increasing tourism. Web sites, television commercials, brochures, bumper stickers, colorful publications, and coffee mugs are just a few of the publicity items that states have designed to attract tourism. Themes such as "Wake Up to Missouri" or "Tennessee Sounds Good to Me" are now featured in television commercials. Development of a 30-second commercial can easily cost $10,000 or more. Each time the state commercial is shown on television it costs between $100,000 and $1 million, but it's money well spent.

Most people associate sandy beaches or ski slopes with tourism. Florida, California, Colorado, and Texas are frequent vacation spots for spring breaks and family vacations. Increasingly, however, states one might not think of as vacation destinations seek tourist dollars. Many northern states without ski resorts spend their advertising budgets from March through September, realizing that many families take summer vacations. Cities like Ames, Iowa have attracted popular country music festivals. Iowa State's football stadium sells out for the popular music festival and the economy benefits from tourism. Hotels fill with out-of-town guests, and restaurants pump up their volume of business.

Thousands of travelers pass through Nebraska each year and few of them stop as they speed through to South Dakota's Black Hills or Colorado's Rocky Mountains.

Nebraska State Senator Roger Wehrbein wants Nebraska to be a destination. He has proposed a bill to annually set aside $1.5 million in general funds for developing Nebraska's tourism industry. Attractions like the Henry Doorly Zoo in Omaha, the Great Platte River Road Archway Monument, Nebraskaland Days, and the Burwell Rodeo could all become more popular tourist attractions with a little extra money for advertising. Iowa, Nebraska's main competitor in the tourism industry, spends $17 million annually on tourism development while Nebraska spends just $2.7 million.

Developing the state's tourism industry would lead to new jobs and increased revenue for the state in urban and rural areas. This example from Nebraska demonstrates the value of tourism to local economies. Multiply that by the fifty states vying for the tourist dollar, and you begin to see the economic impact. Not only are tourist dollars essential for the hospitality industry, there is a ripple effect, as advertising jobs, media development, and travel businesses from airlines to gas stations also depend on the motion of visitors from one place to another.

Travel Packages

A travel package is a prearranged vacation. Some packages include basic travel services, while others may include a complete travel plan. Usually these packages are assembled by independent tour operators and are sold through travel agents. Purchasing a travel package has the advantage of convenience and value. A vast array of travel packages can cause confusion, so it is extremely important to read the fine print in advertisements and contracts. All extra charges should be clearly and conspicuously disclosed. It is also important to research tour operators to determine if they are reliable. Recommendations from friends and relatives can provide assurance. The Better Business Bureau may also provide valuable information.

International Tourism

Astrong global economy in 2000 and special events to celebrate the new millennium resulted in a 7.4% increase in world tourism. This growth doubled the increase of 1999. International trips increased by 50 million in 2000. This is the same number of new tourists that major countries such as Spain or the United States receive in the entire year. The World Tourism Organization (WTO) estimated a record 698 million international travelers in 2000. Receipts from international tourism totaled $476 billion. All regions of the world hosted more tourists in 2000. The fastestgrowing regions included East Asia and the Pacific.

The strong dollar and weak European currency attracted record numbers of American tourists to Europe, with Germany and Switzerland enjoying their best results in years. The Middle East was on a fast track of increased tourism before renewed violence cut the flow of tourists to the region. International tourism goes two ways, of course. Even with a strong dollar, the United States attracted millions of additional international tourists and achieved an 8.7% growth rate. Economic slowdown in the United States and other key locations throughout the world reduces international tourism.

7

Customer Relationship Management

Mass production as a paradigm of management has dominated the world industrial production since World War II, and it has fettered the tremendous growth in American economy in the twentieth century. With shifting demographics and changing consumer tastes and preferences, mass production for homogeneous markets is not enough to keep businesses going.

Mass customization is arising in direct response to the turbulence that has splintered the mass market. One sharp-eyed observer who spotted the coming of mass customization long ago is perhaps United States' best known futurist, Alvin Toffler. As far back as 1970, Toffler wrote in Future Shock about "destandarized" goods and services that he forecast the United States would produce in "great variety." Speaking recently to INC by telephone, Toffler said that mass customization will proceed with a kind of gravitational force because, as American become more affluent, they have wanted greater individuality. People now can afford it partly because technology makes it cheaper. Michael Cox, chief economist at the Federal Reserve Bank of Dallas, in concurrence with Toffler lamented that "If you don't customize, you're going to lose business in today's marketplace."

Nowadays, virtually all companies recognize the need to be customer driven by providing superior service to satisfy customers' needs. But as customers and their needs grow increasing diverse, unnecessary cost and complexity are inevitably added to operations. Companies around the world have embraced mass customization in an attempt to avoid those pitfalls of trying to meet every customer's need. Readily available information technology and flexible processes permit them to customize goods or services for individual customers in high volumes and at a relatively low cost.

Mass Customization

Mass customization is neither a simple strategy to undertake organizationally and operationally, nor is it a simple concept to comprehend. Hart defined mass customization by using two distinct definitions: The visionary definition: The ability to provide customers with anything they want profitably, any time they want it, anywhere they want it, any way they want it.

According to Hart, the goal in the first definition will rarely be achieved by an organization. It was considered a transcendent, absolute idea that exists solely as an ideal. The goal in the second definition is not the "anything-at-any-time" promised by the visionary definition. It is "to ascertain, from the customer's perspective, the range within which a given product or service can be meaningfully customized (i.e. differentiated) for that customer, and then to facilitate the customer's choice of options from within that range." He lamented that the concept of producing tailor-made or partially tailor-made goods or services according to customer desire, with very short cycle times and mass production efficiencies, is a more realizable goal than that offered by the visionary definition.

In essence, mass customization is a hybrid technique by which a company churns out products in typical assembly-line fashion yet can add unique features to individual orders. This requires a flexible manufacturing system that anticipates a wide range of options. However, due to the vast differences in customer preferences, mass customization, too, can produce unnecessary cost and complexity. Therefore, it is crucial that managers must examine thoroughly what kind of customization their customers would value before they adopt this new strategy.

Hart further identified four key decision factors:

1. *Customer sensitivity*: The first question companies need to ask themselves is: Do your customers care whether you offer more customization? If the answer is no, the mass customization potential is limited.
2. *Process amenability*: This is a multifaceted area. The first obvious question is: Does your process technology, which exists in your area allow you to customize your product or service to individual customers? If it does, the next question is how extensive an overhaul is required to incorporate this technology into your existing process and how much investment will be required? Another part of process amenability is marketing. Since the goal of mass customization is products or services tailored to individual customers, an important question for companies to ask is: Does the marketing department have access to the level of detail regarding customer needs and the capacity to analyze such information? A third consideration is design. Is your company capable of translating custom needs into actual specifications? The last consideration under this factor is production and distribution. Partly depending on the form and nature of product or service, the flexibility of the production system to handle mass customization is a critical point here.
3. *Competitive environment*: The major question here is: Are there competitive forces that would enhance or detract from the advantage your company would gain from implementing mass customization? In other words,

would you be the first in your market with a mass-customized product? How long would it take for competitors to react? And how will your competitors' customers react?

4. *Organizational readiness*: The last decision factor requires an honest assessment of your company's culture and resources. Is your company able and ready to capitalize on the opportunity inherent in mass customization? Organizational change requires enlightened leadership, open-minded management, and financial resources. Hence, mass customization strategy is unique to the company developing and implementing it. There is no "cookie-cutter" approach to creating such a strategy. Mass customization strategy that works for one company might not work for another company.

In 1997, Gilmore and Pine identified four distinct approaches to customization, which are collaborative, adaptive, cosmetic, and transparent. They advocated that when designing or redesigning a product, process, or business unit, managers should choose an approach or a mix of some or all of the four approaches to serve their own particular set of customers.

1. *Collaborative customization*: This approach follows three steps: first to conduct a dialogue with individual customers to help them articulate their needs; second, to identify the precise offering that fulfills those needs; and third, to make customized products for them. Collaborative customization is most appropriate for businesses whose customers cannot easily articulate what they want and grow frustrated when forced to select from a plethora of options.
2. *Adaptive customization*: Adaptive customizers offer one standard, but customizable, product that is designed so that users can alter it themselves. This approach is appropriate for businesses whose customers want the product to perform in different ways on different

occasions, and available technology makes it possible for them to customize the product easily on their own.

3. *Cosmetic customization*: This approach is appropriate when customers use a product the same way and differ only in how they want it presented. in other words, the standard offering is packaged specially for each customer.
4. *Transparent customization*: This approach is appropriate when customers' needs are predictable or can easily be deduced, and especially when customers do not want to state their needs repeatedly. Offerings were customized within a standard package for individual customers.

To sum up, collaborative customizers change the product itself in addition to changing some aspect of the presentation while a cosmetic customizer changes only the presentation of the product. A transparent customizer uses a standard representation to mask the customization of the product and finally adaptive customizers change neither the product nor the representation of the product but they provide the customer with the ability to change both the product's function and/or its presentation to meet their needs.

Fast-food

Fast-food restaurants and other McDonaldized systems are mass production systems, which were built upon the belief that in the world of mass production, consumers accept homogeneous products. Their acceptance facilitates market growth and the reduction of prices through economies of scale, which in turn leads to a greater price gap between mass-produced goods and that of customized goods. As with other mass producers, the fast-food industry has reached the limited of the old paradigm. In 1995, Taylor and Lyon reported mass customization as an alternative to

McDonaldization. They recognized that fast-food companies, including McDonald's, have experienced the same sources of discontinuity as other mass producers, creating extreme pressure for change.

Burger King was the first one to embrace the principles of mass customization - "Have it your way!" and "Sometimes you've gotta break the rules!" The focus then was on burgers and fries but later shifts testified that this was only the start. Using McDonald's as an example, it can be seen that standardization is still a characteristic of its operations. However, its menu has been expanded not only to suit local tastes and preferences but also to offer more variety. Pizza, fajitas, breakfast burritos, submarine sandwiches, spaghetti and meatballs, carrot and celery sticks were included in some menus. Internationally, for McDonald's in France the menu is written in three to five different languages, usually, French, German, Italian, Belgian, and Japanese.

Some menu items, which are offered in France, are not available in the United States. These items are bagels, red seasoned potato wedges with dipping sauce, cakes and pastries, scones and croissants. The drinks offered are also different. Dr. Pepper and root beer are not offered while Orangina, an orange flavored carbonated drink, beer and wine are available for purchase. For the breakfast menu, McDonald's in France also offers a fruit salad and scones. Salad and dessert choices are also varied, as the chef salad is served with salmon and shrimp, and eclairs, brownies, muffins, and beignets are included in the dessert menu. Pork is not used in Muslim nations. Big Macs in India are prepared with mutton. Soups are offered in Hong Kong operations.

Beverage cup sizes are much smaller in Asian countries' McDonald's, and there is no refill. One may argue that this is product differentiation, but why do we differentiate product? To suit customers' needs! For

McDonald's to have radically expanded it output variety, it underwent a paradigm shift characterized by shorter development and production cycles, flexibility, autonomy, process innovations and the adoption of a true customer focus.

Lodging

It was pointed out that the hospitality industry has generally preferred to keep wages low, thus avoiding the need for technological innovation, particularly in the actual delivery of its services. Although technology has been used extensively in a supporting role to enhance performance and effectiveness, (e.g., computer reservation system, air control technology, accounting system) there has been a great reluctance to replace human service providers with technologically driven alternatives. However, in recent years, some "tinkering" of mass customization has occurred in selected areas in the lodging industry. The new demographic trend suggests new features in the hotel room that caters specifically to the needs and preferences of the senior travelers. These new features, made possible by technology include:

— ergonomically-designed furniture that facilitates standing from a seated position with the aid of a weight/height sensing cushion or provides support to a tired back through sensors that adjust to the most comforting back support;

— blankets that utilize the same fiber technology as found on the space shuttles heat shield and thus will respond to body temperature retaining or expelling heat to maintain a comfortable temperature and more restful night's sleep;

— alarm clocks that awaken the guest to increasing light levels that begin with the light daybreak to a full daylight, for those whose hearing may riot be as sharp as it was in the past.

The applications of virtual reality are also a unique feature of the future hotel room. The project is examining the applications of video walls that would replace or perhaps supplement windows in guest rooms, allowing the room's occupant to select the scenery that would be most complimentary to her/his activity in the room. For the business traveler in the work zone it might be sights and sounds that are most stimulating to the busy executive's productivity, transferring to the entertainment zone with sights and sounds from his/her favorite sporting event or concert; and finally to the relaxation/rest zone, where the stress business traveler can unwind with the sight/sounds of family or a favorite vacation spot.

With all that is said about high-tech, the bottom line is that guests want a room that is comfortable and adaptable to their particular needs. Many guests' expectations are not particularly high-tech. All guests want a good night's sleep which may mean paying attention to the soundness of the mattress being provided: what type of mattress does you guest prefer? According to the Westin sleep study conducted for the chain by a New York-based research firm, the main criticism by 27% of respondents was that hotel mattresses are too soft. For another 21 percent, the number one complaint was that mattresses are too hard. There are two concepts - one utilizing springs and the other air -are being studied that will allow guests to adjust the firmness of each side of a bed. Other than the mattresses, guest of the future hotel room will be provided an assortment of pillows ranging from soft to firm and some or all hypoallergenic.

Industries, which are less dependent on the human interactions have adopted laborsaving technology. As a result, these industries have been able to improve wage levels and enhance career opportunities for employees while keeping costs under control. For example, banks replace human tellers with automatic teller machines, which not only save labor costs but also offer 24-hour service year round. This kind of convenience provided to their customers can be considered a great customization.

Customer Equity

It is often said that you are what you measure, and you measure only what you think is important. The ways that organizations gauge performance reflect their historic roots and basic orientation to creating value. Clearly, that maxim holds true today in the hospitality industry. Our industry has historically measured itself with a standard metric used worldwide - revenue-per-available-room (REVPAR). More than simply a way to quantify results, REVPAR reflects our industry's fundamental structure and value proposition based on physical assets (hotel rooms) as the driver of wealth. With the magnitude of change driven by technology, it is now essential to ask is REVPAR still the best measure of performance for a hotel organization, or does it reflect an outmoded view of a hotel's performance horizon?

Technology is changing every aspect of how we live, work and profit, and it should come as no surprise that technology must also change how the hospitality industry serves customers and measures itself. In short, the "end game" can no longer be REVPAR - revenue measured by the physical asset. The most profitable hotel organizations of the future will be those that capture an increasing share of the customer's purchasing power - while they are in the hotel, at home or anywhere else in the world. What drives this change is technology, which makes it possible to serve customers in both physical place (the hotel room) and virtual space (anytime and anywhere).

The historic measure of hotel performance - REVPAR - must thus give way to a metric that reflects the customer as the more fundamental driver of value in the hospitality industry. Revenue-per-available-customer (REVPAC) does just that. In our contemporary world, hotel organizations are no longer constrained by physical location in serving customers. New media and systems technologies offer extraordinary efficiencies in delivering products and services with greater speed, lower cost and improved flexibility. Furthermore, technology offers unprecedented opportunities for innovation in an industry's changing menu of products and services. What does this mean for our industry? We are witnessing a period of major change as the fundamental value proposition of our industry is overturned.

Customers - not physical assets - drive wealth in all industries, and the hospitality industry is certainly no exception. Technology deployed in enterprise-wide platforms makes it possible to get closer to customers. It provides tangible benefits as it offers opportunities to increase business value, reduce operational costs and create new opportunities for growth in the industry.

At stake is technology's impact on customer equity - defined as the degree to which an industry has fully developed relationships with its customers, providing them with more products and services to meet exiting and emerging needs. REVPAC, as a measure of performance, embodies a shift in perspective from an "asset play" based on hotel properties and rooms to a focus on leveraging customer equity for shareholder wealth.

REVPAC casts a spotlight on a number of key questions for the industry on the eve of the 21st century. How can hotel organizations "talk" to customers in a way they have never been spoken to before by the industry? What must companies do to "hear" their customers in new ways, learning how to better represent them and their needs in the market? How can hospitality organizations maximize revenues by making the most of their relationships with customers? Hotel guests are not lust customers who seek room and board, and perhaps a fax machine in the room. They represent a consumer with an array of needs, whose time is Limited and who, in many cases, will respond to diverse products, improved service and convenience.

In the future, the traditional "marketplace" (the physical realm made up of destinations and hotel buildings) will be greatly expanded to incorporate the virtual environment or "marketspace" - a market context and environment rendered accessible by technology as physical location becomes irrelevant. Understanding the potential of both the marketplace and marketspace sets the stage for delivery of expanded products and services — some traditional, others less so — to customers.

Talking and Listening to Customers

Technology thus plays a key role, both in delivering products and service in virtual space, but also in enhancing the ability to listen and talk with customers in new ways. Sophisticated management information systems allow companies to identify with increasing precision the customer segments and markets that offer the greatest opportunities for growth, given the pace of change in a global economy. A technology platform must incorporate two systems, however, to support the hospitality industry's potential for improving customer equity. Customer reservations systems track when and where customers are going, and what they will do when they get there. Customer information systems track who the customers are, what they purchase, and how they live and work.

Hospitality companies already use reservation systems to get customers into the hotel. Information systems generate customer profiles based on tracking consumption patterns in the process defining a diverse range of wants and needs. This poses a number of challenges. Certainly, it will be important to integrate data generated at the property level with reservations systems and customer information in a total system solution that provides for data warehouses and networked communications. In such a system, customer information is captured from a variety of sources, and becomes the platform for the highly focused marketing and product development strategies of the future.

The hospitality in the industry will thus require two types of infrastructure to do business - real estate and technology - to support a shirt from depending on "place" to a reliance on "space" to fully meet customer needs. This follows a four-stage evolution currently taking place in industries across the board. The hospitality industry, for example, historically focused on developing major physical assets, with an almost exclusive orientation to financing and building individual properties. At this first stage, companies achieved relatively low customer equity, providing a narrow band of products and services, traditional to the hospitality industry, at various physical locations.

As the industry matured, it differentiated itself to meet more diverse customer needs with properties matched to the various market niches. In this second stage, business hotels and all-suite properties are examples of such differentiation. A third stage involves serving customers in ways that do not require a physical address at all, including telephone marketing and catalog sales. And in the fourth state - the age of electronic commerce - the "real estate" is actually owned by the consumers themselves in the form of a personal computer located on a desktop, eliminating the need for many types of businesses to own significant physical assets in order to create wealth.

At each of these stages, the potential for customer equity rises with increased access to customers, regardless of their physical location, while the costs associated with fixed-assets (real estate) declines. The evolutionary track moves from exclusive reliance on major assets to combinations of physical assets and technology in reaching customers. Indeed, new media and systems technologies can be designed to give hotel organizations greatly enhanced access to larger numbers of customers - regardless of physical location. These technology platforms also spawn rapid innovation in products and services, combined with improved speed to market. The result enhanced business valuation and higher stock prices as a company's strategic, technological and financial architectures are aligned to generate customer equity.

Hospitality companies can dramatically improve the valuation of their companies by using new technology to bring them closer to their customers. This is particularly the case with major companies that have not fully served their large customer bases and have good potential to build customer equity. In many cases these organizations are our industry's major franchisors, whose goals are typically to sign up new franchisees and improve the yields from each property. In a nutshell, these companies are using franchising as a growth vehicle and their orientation is to maximizing fee income.

For these organizations, an intermediate performance measure might be described as revenue-per-available-franchisee (REVPAF). The challenge here will be to develop ways to reach the primary customer (hotel guest) directly, rather than simply through the franchisee organizations - with the end game being improved REVPAC. The typical franchisor catches the primary customer in its reservation system, but typically doesn't "speak" to that customer again, either during the guest stay or after leaving the hotel property. Franchisors will benefit as they begin to develop the strategies and systems allowing them direct access to the primary customers, with a goal of increasing REVPAC.

Online Distribution Strategy

Direct-to-consumer online distribution should become the foundation, the main focus of any hotelier's online distribution strategy. In the offline world, hoteliers are the best direct salesmen with an estimated 75% of all reservations sold directly to consumers. Online, the industry direct sales average 52% with many hoteliers reporting less than 5%. As a result, many hoteliers cede control of their inventory and pricing to online intermediaries, at an enormous cost financially and to brand integrity. Website optimization is the first step toward building a robust direct online distribution strategy.

The Internet is the ultimate "Direct Distribution Medium". It provides the hotel with long-term competitive advantages by lessening dependence on intermediaries, online discounters and traditional channels that may soon become obsolete. Any promising, sustainable, and defensible distribution strategy must start locally at the hotel website. Direct-to-consumer online distribution has the following benefits:

— Puts the hotel in control of its Internet presence and exposure

— Prevents brand and price erosion

— Lessens dependence on online discounters and intermediaries

— Is the shortest path to establishing interactive relationships with customers

— Provides long-term opportunities to benefit from the lifetime customer value

— Is the least expensive way to distribute hotel inventory—direct to consumer!

The foundation of a hotel's direct online distribution strategy begins with the website. A well functioning, fully optimized hotel website is a real asset that serves as the chief instrument to capture new markets and facilitate transactions. Unfortunately a majority of today's hotel websites and web strategies in hospitality suffer from two common flaws:

Websites built with no online distribution strategy: Most hotel websites are performing poorly as far as online distribution and search engine strategy are concerned. Why? Most hotel websites have been developed by web designers who know nothing about the hospitality industry, based on input and concepts by hoteliers who are not experts on Internet strategy, online distribution, and eMarketing. And many of them were designed as online brochures without taking into account fundamental online distribution principles.

Using a "quick fix" approach to undo what's fundamentally wrong: Such hotel websites, built without clear online distribution concepts and principles, inevitably produce poor results and few bookings. Hoteliers then turn to Search Engine Optimization (SEO) vendors for a quick fix of the hotel website to boost search engine rankings and increase online revenues. In reality, "slapping" meta tags to a stale, user-unfriendly website and submitting it to the search engines can achieve few sustainable results.

Only a fully optimized website can produce the desired online revenues and position your hotel company ahead of the competition. Website optimization takes a comprehensive look at the website and prepares it for optimal performance (maximum user experience, bookability and conversion rates) and yes, for the search engines. Especially in hospitality, regaining control of distribution from the online discounters and building a presence over the web directly to consumers is increasingly important. Website optimization is an imperative in today's marketplace.

Hoteliers who have instituted website optimization strategies are ahead of the curve with their own direct distribution strategies. They have higher placement on the search engines and are able to convert more lookers into booker. These hoteliers understand that online consumers prefer to buy directly from the hotel. They recognize the hotel website is a source to control room inventory, hotel descriptions and content, room pricing and availability, group-bookings, and corporate rate programs, something completely unachievable on any third-party channel.

Website Optimization

To begin with, a hotel website is not an online brochure. It is not meant to serve as reference material secondary to a sales pitch. The website is a 24/7 sales and marketing tool, a hotel's top producing "virtual" sales office. The website is a "living organism" with descriptive copy, images and keyword updates, special packages, email capture, and overall fresh and locally relevant information—all meant to enhance the user experience and all easily achievable at minimal cost. Therefore, website optimization addresses eDistribution, revenue management, and overall marketing—well outside the role of web designers and more closely associated with eBusiness experts.

Website optimization consists of several core components that combined reflect best practices. These are: user-friendly website, search engine readiness, website bookability, and eCRM. Several features that characterize a user-friendly website and search engine readiness are identified underneath the headings below.

User-friendly website

— Introduce credible and optimized body copy
— Address the "trust" issue to boost consumer confidence (e.g. Privacy Policy)
— Streamline navigation by introducing well defined, easy-to-use tiered navigation
— Increase conversion rates by introducing a robust real-time booking engine
— Consider offering lowest price guarantee

— Set up search/availability box right on Home Page
— Make all promos and packages bookable in real time
— Optimize images to improve download speeds
— Improve download speeds to less than 15 seconds at 56K ("AOL Benchmark")
— Introduce rich media features: virtual tours, photo shows, floor plans, etc
— Develop sections/pages to target specific customer segments
— Introduce foreign languages to attract foreign clientele
— Utilize low-cost customer support and FAQ
— Offer customer email capture

Website Optimization Blueprint

With general theory out of the way, let's get to work creating a website optimization blueprint. The blueprint drives the entire website optimization strategy and serves as the vehicle to communicate to the team, including web designer, exactly what goes into the website. A well developed blueprint serves as the backbone for the entire direct-to-consumer distribution strategy. The blueprint, built by professionals schooled in online distribution, revenue management, and eMarketing strategies, creates a comfort zone in forming the clarity hoteliers so desperately need. The blueprint nicely bridges the gap between web designers who will eventually implement the blueprint and hoteliers who don't know how to use the Internet as a distribution channel.

From a feasibility standpoint, a website optimization blueprint serves a number of purposes:

Focus on Core Competence: Working off a website optimization blueprint allows the web designer to focus on core skills: the look-and-feel, overall website design, HTML code and website functionality. Building marketing messages, learning online distribution models, and understanding ASP booking engine technologies are left to eBusiness experts.

Competitive Bids: Working from a blueprint, a web designer can easily base an accurate quote on what exactly goes into the website. Price quotes for website design, re-design, or simple implementation are much more precise, usually 25%-40% lower in costs.

Expedited Implementation Process: Once the web designer creates the new look-and-feel, the web development consists of simply cutting and pasting each component of the blueprint into HTML code. The contents of the blueprint have already received management approval.

Bridges the "Knowledge Gap": A majority of hoteliers are not experts in online distribution while web designers do not know hospitality. The optimization blueprint bridges the knowledge gap in best practices as well as prevents unnecessary up-selling by web designers.

Body Copy

The body copy plays an essential role in promoting the hotel to web customers. It is the copy that describes the hotel products, features, room services, amenities, and local destination information. The copy should be truthful and written in short, declarative, and descriptive sentences.

Creating the Keyword List

Creating the keyword list requires a combination of Internet, hospitality and destination-specific knowledge and extensive research. Some required steps include:

— Identify patterns of consumer online purchasing habits for the hotel/resort and the particular destination;

— Destination research to identify relevant copy

— Research to identify relevant target keywords

— Research to rank the keywords according to their popularity
— Develop credible and relevant copy
— Weave the target keywords throughout the copy
— Develop the "invisible copy": page titles, description tags and meta tags.

A major goal of the website optimization process is to leverage the popularity of a particular destination for the benefit of the hotel website. The optimized destination content within a single or multi-market hotel website is very important for the search engines and ongoing marketing including email and pay-per-click campaigns. Scoring top positioning on search engines will depend on how well constructed the word and phrase list reflects your product and destination, and only comes after careful research on consumer search behavior and purchasing habits. Building this list requires software to analyze popularity, word matching to analyze relevancy, bench research to dig out unique and specific words and common phrases to the search that characterize the destination, and finally some human discretion from those with a depth and understanding of online marketing in hospitality and use of search engines.

Guest Response Systems

Throughout the hotel industry, numerous improvement programs exist that focus an organization on defect reduction, customer service and process alignment. Hotels are a fast paced, highly variable working environment where things change constantly. The quantity and type of data collected by a real-time guest response system is far more useful for eliminating defects than data collected from post-visit surveys. When combined with guest defects reported from other sources such as comment cards and surveys, the guest response system helps manage the chaos and creates the foundation of a successful quality management program.

After implementing process improvement with data collected from a real-time guest response system, one hotel saw its problem experience percentage drop from 30 percent to 20 percent in two years. That is equivalent to eliminating one third of all guest problems. Overall guest satisfaction increased dramatically and operating costs decreased because of more efficient operations and reduced guest compensation.

Managers who rely on information gathered anecdotally run the risk of making process changes or financial decisions that lead to misuse of resources and mediocre results. Those who rely on actual defect data and not gut instincts to make decisions about process improvements will be the most successful at improving guest service and satisfaction. The more relevant data one has, the higher the probability that a good decision will be made. There are myriad opportunities to collect guest feedback and defect data: when a reservation is made, at check-in, through the hotel call center, via staff who are confronted face-to-face by guests, at check-out, and from comment cards or any other correspondence that a guest might send after a hotel stay. Most guest response systems focus on the time a guest is in a hotel but some do provide components that enable data collection prior to check-in and after check-out.

A real-time guest response system can track the following types of data: the amount of time it takes to respond to a request by staff, request or department; how many requests or problems are successfully responded to within a specified goal period; and the amount of time it takes to dispatch a call. A guest response system also can generate incident reports by department, an overall top 10 incidents report, predict peak request times to optimize staffing and generate work orders for maintenance personnel.

Maintenance Issues

Maintenance issues can be a big cause of guest problems. Rarely is there a set or predefined time to replace aging equipment or furnishings. By using a defect report, one can pinpoint the optimum time to replace an aging product. Two key factors in determining optimum replacement time are impact on the customer and maintenance costs including labor.

Manage Amenity Requests and Housekeeping

Although typically not viewed as defects, guest requests collected by guest response systems provide a great opportunity for process improvement. These requests can be ranked by type, frequency and cost. One hotel manager used a top 10 requests report to identify a need for two foam pillows in each guestroom. The decision was based on the cost of delivering more than 100 foam pillows per month versus placing them in every room. The labor savings alone made up for the cost of the pillows in one year and hotel staff had more time and resources to deal with other issues. A key consideration when examining amenity requests is the impact on staffing levels and meeting service delivery standards. The fewer the number of requests, the easier it is to shorten the response time for other issues and amenities. In larger hotels and resorts, fewer requests can reduce the number of runners required to meet the standard delivery times.

Guest response reports also can reveal trends based on variables other than overall request frequency such as day of the week or time of day graphs. One convention hotel's staff in Orlando discovered that requests for extra towels were much higher for certain groups and on the weekends. Based on the data the decision was made to add guestroom towels during those occasions. The result was an improvement in overall average response times because runners no longer had to address the towel shortage problem. Similar logic can be applied to other amenities based on the season or room type.

GuestWare is a guest response system that enables one to break housekeeping incidents down by section. By analyzing a graph in one such report, a hotel's manager discovered that housekeepers had been flushing used soap down guestroom toilets. The soap caused flushing problems. The soap disposal process was changed and the problems stopped. Similar reports also can be used to monitor other housekeeping-related issues such as dirty rooms or broken coffee pots. One hotel determined that certain housekeepers were breaking coffee pots during cleaning. The problem was resolved in one meeting and eliminated from the top 10 list altogether.

Guest Response Systems

In hotels where guest response systems are not used, a measurement such as average response time is difficult, if not impossible, to track. If you cannot measure it, you cannot manage it. Sometimes the simple act of tracking response time can motivate employees to respond more rapidly to requests and problems. Average response time and goal analysis (percentage of calls within the goal) are each helpful metrics that improve processes. Reviewing these for each request type, by runner, by time of day and by day of week can shed light on problems and inspire potential solutions. A common use of this information is to shift staffing levels to maintain delivery standards.

Analyzing average response time by problem type can provide insight into training and organization improvements. Simple things like creating well positioned storage closets for the top 10 issues can shave 5 percent to 10 percent off response time. Similarly, knowing what tools are needed for each task can prevent an employee from making two separate trips.

8

Web-based Marketing Strategies

A retrospective view of how high technology has been used in the hospitality industry reveals the depth of change wrought in hotel operations during the past four decades. Accounting and financial systems were introduced during the 1960s, but exclusively as mainframe-based systems operated by the largest hotels. Systems oriented to property management were introduced in the 1970s. During the 1980s, systems were ported to mini-computer and micro-computer based platforms. Accounting, financial and property management systems finally became available even to the smallest operators. Sales and marketing applications were developed to provide a competitive advantage for properties.

The technology life cycle provides a model to assess how and when companies and individuals adopt new technologies. Investments in technologies can generate greatly improved operating efficiencies, higher hotel revenues and enhanced guest services. The pace of change, however, has been so extreme as to leave many hotel organizations uncertain about what types of technology to adopt and the best ways to create a seamless integration of systems company-wide. Many hotel organizations are using technologies so outdated as to place their companies at a competitive disadvantage in the marketplace.

High-tech or high-touch is largely a thing of the past in the hospitality industry as emerging technologies drive unprecedented change in the way hotels operate and serve customers. Pioneers are generally the first to acquire new technologies and take the greatest risk. A second category of technology users — leaders — adopt relatively unproven technologies, but the risks are known and accepted. Obsolete technology at the other end of the spectrum may seriously impair a company's ability to compete. In terms of costs and benefits, the best balance appears to be with the leaders who invest significantly less than pioneers and incur reduced risks, yet their technology investments can yield similar benefits.

Finding that balance in technology investment is critical today for hotel operations, given its importance in two areas:

— The desire of operators to improve the guest experience. This is demonstrated through faster check-in and check-out, more timely response to service requests and a myriad of other opportunities to enhance services.

— The potential to improve operating efficiencies. Hotel operators are seeking ways to reduce staffing requirements, cross-train staff, reduce the overall general and administrative expense, and explore opportunities for centralizing some functions while at the same time distributing other functions more widely.

Implementing technological advances promises the potential for greatly enhanced guest services to meet rising customer expectations, improved cost control, more effective marketing strategies and expanded opportunities for hotel companies and properties to achieve a competitive advantage. However, technology is only as good as its application by an organization, and therein lies the challenge for hospitality companies‹weighing how best to invest in technology, as well as train employees and implement its use.

The 1990s will be marked as the decade of integration, driven by powerful networking capabilities offered by client server technology. This technology will bring no less than the dismantling of the management information system (MIS) paradigm as we have known it, more completely democratizing access to information than at any time in the past.

Client Server Technology

Client server computing currently has no standard, agreed-upon definition. Generally, however, the client server architecture involves "integrated, networked computer systems using applications cooperating across the network," according to Stewart Alsop of InfoWorld. Instead of having a series of mainframes networked together, client server architectures involve one large processor unit and a network of clients linked together, often across large geographic areas. Client server systems make the best use of both the networked client computers processing and user interface abilities, and the server systems database, computational and data management abilities.

Client server architectures offer major benefits to companies adopting these systems. Data access is faster because the "server" is not burdened with running applications. Data access is more evenly distributed, and users have the ability to query and create their own reports. At the same time, design of the database can be truly independent of the applications, which are run on the "user" computers.

Client server technology in the hospitality industry offers significant opportunities as companies make decisions relating to technology. In addition to improving services, hotel operators are seeking ways to effectively integrate the disparate systems accumulated during the last decade. Most of the larger hotel properties currently are running multiple computer platforms (systems), and due to the cost of technology, will continue to do so for the next several years. These platforms have evolved from a patchwork of tactical solutions initiated by various functional areas. Client server technology is probably the most viable strategic option for medium to large multi-property owners and operators as technology upgrades are made.

The number of enterprises in general industry that have adopted client server architectures, for example, has risen from 35 percent in 1992 to more than 60 percent today, according to the research firm, International Data Corporation. Similar levels of use can be expected in the hospitality industry. Client server technology benefits hotel organizations primarily because it "decouples" the applications from the database contained on the "server"system. In practical terms, this means that the applications typically used in the hospitality industry can be developed by different vendors (as is typically the case), yet use a common database. Ad hoc reporting and MIS support are simplified and more efficient.

The client server approach, then, makes it possible to rebuild an information technology (IT) infrastructure to unify mainframes, midrange systems and PCs with universal connectivity in a single infrastructure as the ultimate goal. Optimally, hotel organizations should be able to reduce IT costs, leverage investments in PCs and improve staff productivity. In addition, client server technology sets the stage for the still more sophisticated technologies of the next decade in which guests will have greater access to in-room technologies, and fully integrated systems using a common database will be the norm.

Guest Services

For most hotel operations, client server technology is inevitable. The benefits of integration via networked computer systems are compelling given the impact of improved technologies and the opportunity for business process reengineering. At the same time, older technologies are phasing out, and hotel operators will need well-integrated systems to support the database marketing and guest services required to compete in coming years. These include:

One-Stop Services

These services in the hospitality industry have two different applications. Guest services accessed by the guest typically involve the use of the in-room television remote control to select from a suite of interactive programs and services. Guests can navigate easily through multi-media video and audio, and be automatically connected by phone to outside services. In addition, guest services provided by the staff typically involve a PC running a front-end application that allows access to outside services, as well as access to guest-specific information maintained in a central repository or database. In either case, the method employed is driven by the guest familiarity and comfort in using technology.

In the future, one-stop integrated systems will make the same basic services available to hotel staff available to the guest by means of fully integrated systems (retail, ticketing, reservations, etc.) using a central guest data repository and access to outside service providers. All these functions will be on-line and presented to the employee and guest in an intuitive graphical user interface.

Smart Cards

These cards contain an integrated circuit that can allow a guest access to the room or other services in the hotel. Smart Cards also have the potential to be coded for use in charging retail items, meals, minibar use or other purchases. In the future, travel agencies ultimately may issue Smart Card itineraries rather than paper ones. Airlines will have a reader that verifies the traveler's flight number and seat assignment. Hotels will have a reader that can encode the card for use as a room key and capture frequent guest program information.

Since the Smart Card will be a universal card, it could be used at different airlines and hotels during the same trip. The main drawback of Smart Cards currently is standards. Vendors write information in their own coded software which can only be understood by their own reader. Further agreement on standards will need to be reached by the various manufacturers before the power of this technology can be fully exploited.

Video Check

For these services, touch screens on free-standing terminals at kiosks are being developed as part of systems to check in and check out guests without the need to use the traditional front desk. Touch-and-Go, the first system of its kind in the industry, provides the guest who has an advance reservation and a credit card the option of avoiding the front desk at the beginning or end of the stay. Touch-and-Go was successfully tested by Hyatt Hotels at two properties and is now being rolled out to between twenty and thirty of their properties. The target speed for the system is to allow guests to check themselves into their own rooms in less than 90 seconds. The system on check-out allows a guest to approve expenses which appear on-screen, and then print a folio of charges.

Database

At the core of technology-driven marketing is the ability to better target a hotel's customer base. A hotel's customer information file provides the opportunity to segment customers, develop profiles of frequent guests, target prospective customers and improve retention. Many finer hotels maintained a guest history system manually before the advent of affordable computer systems. However, these manual systems were limited in their ability to serve as the basis for a marketing program, and also did not permit the chain operator to identify the best individual customers who frequented multiple hotels within the chain. Client server technology now permits a hotel chain to maintain one single customer database which can be accessed by all of the properties connected to the server over the network. In addition, far more data can be collected about the customer and his spending, making the database much more powerful as a focused marketing tool.

Executive Information Systems (EIS)

These systems offer a way to extract information from disparate systems and present it in a usable and informative manner to top management. What is required is a front-end interactive interface which displays and queries the back-end database (common repository of information) and feeder systems, which include existing financing and operational systems. Design and implementation of an EIS system is typically complex, requiring close examination of a hotel operation's key performance indicators, information sources and other system design features. Once created and implemented, however, an EIS system has the capacity to provide management with a user-friendly, readily accessible and current view of a hotel operation's key financial results and performance indicators.

Technological advances thus have the potential to generate a range of benefits critical to remaining competitive, and ultimately driving expanded market share and profitability. Nevertheless, the barriers to increased investments in technology by hotel owners and operators can be daunting. These include general resistance to change, lack of available funds or manpower to invest in technology, and a perceived inability to quantify benefits.

Like other service companies, hotels are by their very nature more reliant on information than many other industries. The success or failure of a service company can be directly tied to the accuracy of data contained in databases and the speed of retrieval. Clearly, technological advances applied in the hospitality industry will set increasingly higher standards for guest services and hotel operations‹with customer expectations continuing to accelerate. As a result, investments in technologies and effective application of these technologies in hotel operations and services will become one of the most decisive factors differentiating successful hotel organizations globally in the years ahead.

Web Marketing by Tourism

The development and strategic exploitation of the Internet has transformed the basis of marketing. The emergence of agent technology will fundamentally change the interface between the customer and the hotel Web site. Currently, intelligent agents are the focus of intense interest in the field of artificial intelligence and are described as the "new revolution in software". Hotels will need to be aware of agent technology and how agents can be used to promote hotel products in the global electronic market.

The Web as "a perfect medium for selling travel". According to HOTEL's 1998 Worldwide Technology Survey, 81% of hoteliers worldwide were thought to be capable to accept reservations over the Web in 1999. There is now widespread acceptance of the use of the Web for electronic commerce. The Web's potential as a low-cost distribution channel is having a profound effect on both business and consumers. There are a number of reasons for this. The costs for establishing and hosting a Web site vary greatly depending upon the scope of the project, but can be relatively low. The Web offers the possibility of high-speed global information transfer, high levels of interaction and links to computerised reservation and database systems, irrespective of geography, time zone, or computer system. There are therefore benefits in extending the firm's marketing reach to the global marketplace; supplanting traditional distribution channels, and allowing potential consumers browsing time by use of Web technology.

The Web are a possibility for all hoteliers and therefore the Web has the ability to provide equality of access and strategy for all. In addition for larger companies the Web offers a competitive alternative to more traditional computerised distribution channels, such as the Global Distribution Systems. The hotel industry is information-intensive and the Internet is, first and foremost, an information resource. Internet multimedia technology allows for the transmission of sophisticated digital images, video and sound. Hotel "electronic brochures" can now include moving, three-dimensional pictures of the property and facilities, which the potential customer could explore continuously. Virtual hotel tours can now be found on a number of hotels Web sites and views from selected rooms could be simulated. Ticketmaster Online uses such innovation to provide a unique service that shows the view its customers can expect from their theatre seats, fostering one-to-one relationships with customers.

From the marketing perspective a major benefit of the Web is the greater degree of interactivity than other communication media. The most valuable Web applications are those that allow companies to transcend communication barriers and establish dialogue directly with customers. For example, hotel Web sites can contain electronic forms for customer completion and hotels can reply directly via electronic mail (e-mail). This kind of connection will improve customer relations and contribute towards the building of customer loyalty. The Web can give access to a greater store of information than other traditional communication media, and provide visitors with the means to select and retrieve only that which appeals to them. This means that customised brochures, itineraries and guides could be produced at the touch of a key. For the hotels, it provides a useful tool in their adoption of micro marketing in this "Age of the Individual" and relationship marketing. However, it must be remembered that the true determinant is the capability and willingness of customers to use the Web to book hotel rooms and to search for hotel information.

Relationship Marketing

A new form of marketing has emerged as relationship marketing. Various other terms have been used either as substitutes for RM or to describe some close parallel - micro-marketing, loyalty marketing, one-to-one marketing, wrap-around marketing, customer partnering, symbiotic marketing and interactive marketing. Gummesson supports the view that RM represents a "new marketing paradigm" and the beginnings of a new theory. Evans and Laskin suggest: "RM is a customer centered approach whereby a firm seeks long-term business relations with prospective and existing customers". Similarly, Brodie, and Coviello et al have described the major changes taking place in the continuing transition to relationship marketing.

Some critics of RM suggest that it is really no more than a series of transactions over time. Strong rebuttal comes from Czepiel, who argues that a relationship possesses "mutual recognition of some special status between exchange partners". Barnes adds to this by saying that "a succession of interactions does not necessarily lead to a relationship any more than repeat purchasing constitutes loyalty". True marketing relationships, like other human relationships, should be characterised by the deeper feelings of trust, concern and commitment.

In the current competitive market place hotel companies have found it necessary to win the loyalty of the reduced number of customers. As such they need to reorient their thinking away from merely attracting customers to retaining customers. Buttle notes that there are the direct costs of the successful conversion of prospect into a customer as well as the costs of unsuccessful prospecting. Thus, keeping customers loyal is a sensible business strategy. Even with successful campaigns, companies still face the risk of customers defecting, i.e. stop coming back. Defection rates affect retention rates, which is a central issue in relationship marketing. Price Waterhouse calculated that a 2% increase in customer retention is equivalent to a 10% reduction in costs.

There is growing awareness of the lifetime value of customers. A transaction-orientated view of the customer would consider the sales value and margin earned from a single sale, while a relationship-orientated view considers the revenue and contributions earned from a long-term relationship with a customer. Gilbert argues that the lifetime value of retaining customers enables the costs of conversion of the prospect to be set against the revenues earned over the long term. Sales and profits will also improve in direct proportion to the length of time a relationship lasts. In addition, existing customers tend to make more frequent visits, may broaden the base of their own purchases over time, and influence others through word-of-mouth advertising.

A relationship marketing paradigm is most suitable when:

- there is an ongoing or periodic desire for service on the part of the customer;
- the service customer controls the selection the service supplier;
- there exists alternative choice of suppliers;

— word-of-mouth is an especially potent form communication about a product;

— brand switching is a common phenomenon;

— there is an ability to cross sell products.

These characteristics are typical of the hotel industry. RM can also be considered as particularly suitable for the hotel industry because of the ease with which the industry can adopt it. Hotels already possess important customer data from accommodation bookings and the registration process. It is also possible for hotels to retrieve other valuable information from hotel records, such as frequency of stay and spending behaviour. This data can be organised in a database system and manipulated to identify and target customers directly. Hotels are then in an ideal position to begin a relationship with customers.

RM for Hotel and Tourism

The objective of relationship marketing is customer retention. Various hotel and tourism marketing academics have proposed alternative strategies for achieving it. Gilbert proposed that the long-term retention of customers requires the following five steps:

Identify more about the customer through database analysis: The role of the hotel Web site would be to compile information on an individual's purchases or desires, using an incentivised on-line questionnaire. The Web could also track and measure customers reactions to different offers posted on the hotel Web site. Customer profiles could then be created.

Improve and make the product/service more attractive: Again, customised on-line questionnaires could be targeted to frequent guests to collect their attitudes to services or loyalty programmes. The hotel company could use this information to improve aspects of the service that are not meeting or exceeding the expectation of customers. In addition, lapsed or inactive hotel customers could be cost-efficiently contacted using e-mail.

Inform to build customer's knowledge of the company: The Web could serve as a strategic information centre. Key information, such as lists and locations of key agents, as well as hotel company updates on new products, services, offers and benefits, could all be posted on the hotel Web site. Electronic newsletters could also be e-mailed to both prospective and loyal customers. In this mariner, customers will have increased knowledge of the hotel company, which could enhance customer brand loyalty.

Tempt customers to purchase more regularly, try different products, etc: The Web could be used to implement this objective by the direct c-mailing of special electronic promotion leaflets to frequent hotel guests. Furthermore, the hotel Web site could be designed to cross-sell other hotel products/services.

Retain the customer by developing different forms of loyalty schemes: Inspired by the success of the airlines' frequent-flier programmes, hotels have started their own frequent-stayer programmes or customer loyalty schemes. A Web site could be designed for the exclusive use of hotel loyalty scheme members. Entry into the Web site is restricted through the use of identification numbers and passwords. Member's only magazines and special offers could be posted on these exclusive Web pages. Various customer services could also be offered, again exclusively to members. For example, the members of Sheraton's loyalty programme, Sheraton Club International, can keep track of their account activity and redeem rewards on-line.

Gilbert's model can also be considered within the context of criteria for a successful Web strategy advocated by the Butler Group, which advises organisations to:

— treat the Internet as a new medium and exploit its unique properties, such as interaction with customers;

— start with customers by defining who they are and what they want to know;

— build relationships with customers by getting to know them, customising content for them and ensuring relevance to them;

— build a service, not a Web site by giving customers value for time and money and by providing options not available elsewhere;

— leverage existing business by building on assets (brand names, operational infrastructure, information, customer relationships); and

— think radically to achieve the best chance of obtaining the benefits offered by the technology.

It is interesting that each stage of the model encompasses an additional feature, recommended by the Butler group, for a successful Web strategy.

RM and Multimedia

Gilbert's table reveals that as customers are led through the phases of RM, there is an increasing need to convert 'surfing' into a business transaction and to encourage repeat Web site visits. Audience involvement is known to be an essential consideration for successful marketing. However, there is scant research available to indicate how the Web's multimedia characteristics can be used to induce effective marketing communication. The Web offers an alternative, single tool as an integrated communication medium. There is general awareness and understanding of the marketing value of the Web's interactive characteristics, but the effects of multimedia attributes remain under researched.

Furthermore, the problems associated with bandwidth and slow delivery are additional inhibitors to the wide-scale application of multimedia. However, some researchers advocate its use. The use of multimedia on the Web home page is able to upgrade the product or service image and facilitate sales. It is likely that future compression technology and network infrastructure will provide a platform capable of rapid delivery of full media Web sites. It is also reasonable to suggest that multimedia could be used to foster a high involvement condition in hotel customers, encouraging transaction involvement and repeat Web site visits.

It is therefore a matter of importance that the hotel industry considers the effect of Web style, particularly in the domain of sound, video and animation. The hotel industry is information-intensive and the sheer volume of information available will become an increasing burden to consumers. Pattie Maes addresses this problem and predicts that 'programs that can act independently will ease the burdens that computers put on people'. She further speculates that "if untrained consumers are to employ future computers and networks effectively, direct manipulation will have to give way to some form of delegation. Instead of exercising complete control, people will be engaged in a co-operative process in which both human and computer agents initiate communication, monitor events and perform tasks to meet a user's goals.'

Net-based Tourism

Travel and tourism products are ideal for marketing on the Internet. This is because tourism is an information-intensive industry and the Internet is the most effective and efficient means in information exchange worldwide., The Net can greatly facilitate the promotion and distribution of tourist products and potentially enable tourism destinations and enterprises to compete on a level playing field.

Information-Intensive Industry

Tourism is very information-intensive and information is

often dubbed the "life-blood" or "cement" of the industry which holds together the different producers within the travel industry - airlines, tour operators, travel agencies, attractions, car rental, cruise lines, and other supplies. "In few other areas of activity are the generation, gathering, processing, application and communication of information as important for day-to-day operations as they are for the travel and tourism industry". The perishability of tourism products and the often erratic tourist demand make the task of balancing tourism supply and demand far more significant than any other sector. That is probably why tourism became one of the first industries to widely apply IT and conduct electronic commerce from the 1960s in the form of computer(ised) reservation systems (CRSs) and then global distribution Systems (GDSs).

However, the traditional CRSs and GDSs had only improved the information communication between tourist businesses, originally between airlines and travel agents, as they do not directly interact with consumers. The systems are also expensive to both the tourism producer and the retailer. For instance, the GDS cost accounted for an average 8.1% of the International Air Transport Association (IATA) member airlines' distribution cost in 1996 (IATA 2000), and the major GDSs charge around US$600 a month to put a terminal in a travel agency. Moreover, the systems are flawed with incompatibility between each other, especially in the lodging sector, where "switch" companies such as THISCO was needed to connect hotels with all the major GDSs to facilitate room reservations by travel agencies worldwide.

With the effective use of the Internet, these problems can be addressed effectively and cheaply. In addition to its traditional function, a web-based GDS can increase the speed of information transmission, improve the quality of information delivery, reduce the cost to the user as no special connections are necessary, and most important of all, has the potential to interact with all web users in the world.

Having realised the tremendous potential of the Internet, GDS companies already started to develop new and web-based systems which could transform the whole tourism distribution landscape in the near future. For example, Amadeus launched Amadeus Pro Web in January 2000, which is a browser-based reservation tool allowing travel agents to service customers worldwide without a dedicated communications line and at a greatly reduced cost. In fact, with this system any Internet user can become an online travel agent within a week.

Difficult for Tourists to Grasp and Evaluate

As a service industry, most tourist products are intangible services, they are experienced and cannot be touched, tasted, smelt or seen and therefore difficult for tourists to grasp and evaluate. Furthermore, the spatial fixity of tourist attractions and amenities means that a tourist cannot really assess their quality until he arrives at the destination. Tourists have, for a long time, relied on limited information from holiday brochures and other literature to evaluate tours and destinations. Comprehensive, relevant, timely and accurate information is essential in tourists' holiday decision making process. But they were not readily available to tourists until the emergence of the Internet, especially the wide use of the Web.

With the Internet, virtually unlimited amount of information can be stored at a web site and an unlimited number of users can retrieve it at any time from anywhere in the world. The Web can not only provide more information but also provide it from a much wider range of sources; while in the past, tourists are almost exclusively dependent upon representations and descriptions by the travel trade. The Web can also deliver the information in a greater variety of formats, from text to photos, graphs, audio and video clips, whereas in the past, tourists primarily relied on the printed brochures as the limited copies of videos of a limited number of tourism destinations or holidays were only available to the major travel agents.

The web-based electronic brochure can also facilitate the complex process of choosing among the hundreds of holidays using browser-generated selections from back-end databases linked to web servers whereas the printed brochures are usually arranged and indexed by one way, often by destination. Through Internet video telephony, tourists can also "test drive" a prospective holiday by viewing real-time scenes through cameras placed in hotels, clubs, restaurants, scenic spots and other sites in the destination and transmitted via the Internet. Video clips can also show episodes and scenes of festivals, art performances and service delivery to facilitate tourists in the comparison and evaluation of intangible services, the quality of which is otherwise difficult to assess in advance.

Since in tourism, it is the tourists who travel to the destination, rather than the tourist product be transported to the market. When a tourist books an airline seat, a hotel room, or a package holiday, he acquires the right to use that seat, room or holiday in the specified time period. After the tourist completed his journey or holiday, he takes nothing home but experiences. In the whole process, from the booking, through the out journey to the return journey, the only things being transported are travel tickets and the tourist himself. This unique characteristic offers tourism a great advantage in Internet marketing as the only cost of online sale will be the transaction processing expense plus a little postage cost; in contrast, for manufactured goods, the delivery cost is often substantial.

'With the increasing popularity of electronic-ticketing (c-ticketing) or ticketless-travel, especially among airlines, online tourism distribution over the Web may one day have no physical goods to deliver at all. Ticket-less travel means that check-in is achieved by proof of identity and a booking reference number. This saves the cost of ticketing for the airline which would usually include stationery, printing and postage and speeds up the check-in process at airports by enabling passengers to self check-in at check-in machines with a credit card.

Worldwide, there are more than 30 airlines offer e-ticketing in at least some routes in its networks (IATA 2000). About 60% of United Airlines' passengers are now using c-tickets. British Airways has even announced that from May 2000 travellers will be charged £25 for a printed ticket where e-ticketing is available for the flight. It could also cost the traveller £50 to replace a lost paper ticket. Obviously, c-ticketing is a key development that will accelerate the acceptability and convenience of booking air travel via an on-line travel agent. Since such a web-based e-ticket seller has no physical ticket to deliver, it can potentially sell from anywhere in the world to anyone in the world.

Fragmented Tourism Destination Product

As a place product, tourism includes all the elements a destination has to offer to tourists, including the social, cultural and physical environments as well the "touristic" components of tourism supply such as attractions, transport and lodging facilities, and other travel related services. Pollock highlights the difficulties in tourism destination marketing which are attributable primarily to two factors. First, tourism is fragmented in that while the tourist looks at a holiday as a complete "experience", it is sold in the market place "in bits" as beds, meals, tours, seats, etc. by a plethora of independent suppliers that operate independently of one another. Second, no one agency controls or can deliver content about a destination's tourism product as the marketing of a tourism destination is shared by another plethora of organisations such as tourist information centres, regional tourism boards, national tourism organisations and national tourist offices overseas located in main generating markets.

The Internet provides the effective means for a destination to develop a sustainable electronic "infrastructure" that is capable of establishing a comprehensive and multi-lingual destination web site. This site can present existing and potential tourists with up to date information, from a variety of sources, about the destination in all aspects of tourism - tourist attractions, transportation, accommodation, tour operators, travel agencies, shopping and leisure facilities - as well as the background of its people, culture, history, economy, climate. The master destination database can be integrated through hyperlinks with individual tourism companies as well as with suite of applications which enable tourists to pick and mix to make their own holiday "packages".

As such a mega-site could be the "portal" or the "home page" of the web sites of all tourism enterprises in a destinations, it is a great deal easier for the destination to establish itself in the already crowded web-space. From this first stop-of-call, an visitor can search for all the information he needs to make a decision as to whether to visit the destination, what facilities to use and to arrange for reservations and transactions online. In comparison, with the traditional media, in order to get the relevant information of a destination a tourist often needs to go to a travel agency to get a brochure, to a bookshop to get a guide book, and may also contact the destination's national tourist office to get some promotional literature. Furthermore, the printed literature the tourists get is often outdated while a properly constructed and maintained web site can provide right-to-the-minute information.

Fragmented Tourism Industry

The fragmented tourism industry is also polarised in that on the one hand, there are a few large multinational airlines, tour operators, hotel chains and theme parks; on the other, there are millions of small and often family owned businesses, especially in the travel retailing, tour guiding, hotel and catering sectors. For example, in Scotland the average size of the accommodation establishment in the Bed and Breakfast sector was 2.5 rooms in 1999. For the small tourism enterprises, the Web is probably the first effective and feasible medium for them to carry out professional marketing function beyond the basic sales and operating activities.

The Internet has opened the door for small businesses with little capital to reach a worldwide market. Open access results in lower entry barriers so that virtually anyone can both access and provide content to the Internet. Travel retailing is one of the sectors m the economy that requires very little initial capital investment. The Net also re-defines economies of scale, allowing small firms to achieve low unit costs for products and services in markets dominated by large companies. In the hospitality sector, small firms could also have more cost-effective marketing through the destination's web-site than the printed tourist directory. In essence, the Web "levels the playing field". For this reason, Inkpen goes so far as to praise the Internet as a marketer's "dream" because it enables companies of different sizes to compete on more equal terms.

This analysis also applies to tourism destinations. For example, a strong web presence may substantially increase the exposure of many small and developing destinations in the Western market where the high cost of mass media advertising made such exposure practically impossible in the past. Nevertheless, it must be noted that although it costs little to achieve a web exposure, the development of a fully functional marketing and sales site and especially the promotion of the site to increase visitor numbers require huge investment. Therefore, the Internet provides a level playing field for all sizes of companies only at the point of entry - that is, to establish a web presence.

Internet in Tourism Marketing

The Internet as a marketing media can be of great benefit to virtual all areas of marketing, from marketing research, through market segmentation, targeting and positioning, to the effective use of the marketing mix, and marketing organisation and control.

Marketing research

The Internet does more than automating online business transaction, it can "informate" in that it provides a vast amount of information which was previously unavailable. Marketing is essentially an information-processing activity which links an organisation to the external environment in which it operates. The Internet is an invaluable source of low cost but up-to-date marketing intelligence which can be sourced through a company's own site and other web sites. The Internet is extremely useful in build a customer information database. With the use of proper software such as Aurum Software's Web-Trak it is easy to gather systematic data about all users who visited the company's web site.

This information can be used to identify prospects, understand customer needs and customise resources to give greater levels of service to customers. A database of online transaction histories can be the primary marketing resource of tourism companies, determining what kind of travel products they can deliver, what market segments they serve best, and what is the lifetime value of each customer to the firm. By searching other web sites, a company can get valuable information about market demand, supply, competition and economic, demographic, legislation and technological changes in the domestic and international markets.

Web sites of government agencies, media companies and non-profit organisations usually provide large amount of information free on general issues; while commercial sites are good sources of information on new technologies, best business practices, and industry initiatives. Scanning competitors' home pages helps companies to track competitors' marketing strategies and tactics. For example, from hotel chains' web sites, one can easily locate information about the chains' main business activities, financial performance, new hotel openings and investment plans, and key marketing strategies; whereas airlines' web sites often show such useful data as business and financial analysis, strategic alliance groups, new routes development and fleet expansion plans, frequent flyer programmes and the fares and availability of flights between any two destinations.

Market targeting

An important feature of the Web as a medium is that it is the consumer who is actively searching for information about products or brands in which they are interested. In effect the consumer is "pre-screened" and shows both interest and involvement in visiting the web site. While on the Web, the consumer can also provide instantaneous feedback to the marketer. All the feedback, and indeed, every "click" or "hit" the user makes can be memorised by the web server. Through the application of the IT data mining technique, companies can find patterns within their internal customer data and make sense of data or turn data into meaningful marketing information. For instance, the visitation record of an online brochure may show the total number of hits, the distribution of the hits among the pages and across time, the order of the pages been accessed.

The user's visitation data can be easily combined with user profile information from user registrations through online visit cards or questionnaires and used to uncover the consumers 'interest and the patterns of demand and buying behaviour. This in turn leads to identification of likely target segments, often niches based on specific benefit sought. Armed with such information, organisations can refine their targets and develop specific means to achieve true one - to-one marketing. The appropriate use of user profile and surfing behaviour data can improve the effectiveness and efficiency of market segmentation and targeting.

This is because the traditional approach to market segmentation is often based simplistically on geographical, demographic and economic variables while the psycho, behavioural or lifestyle data is costly to collect and difficult to measure and compare. In Internet marketing, it is easier to collect these data from potentially each and every user of the company web site, though tangible rewards such as free prize draws and free membership, are often needed to attract users to fill in web forms. It is even a great deal simpler and more effective in market targeting as the email messages and even tailor-made web-pages can reach the intended receiver with little cost. It is possible to set up 'virtual" or cyber - communities for each target market niche in the form of news-groups through which consumers with similar interest and behaviour patterns can be sent with relevant product offering and other information from the marketer. Members of such Internet communities can regularly exchange information between them and strengthen a sense of belonging.

Product

One of the major advantages of the Internet in marketing is that the tourist can here be a value creator for tourism companies through redefining the labour division between the marketer and the tourist in providing tourist experiences. This is because, on the one hand, tourists can provide individual preferences for or specifications of holiday packages through feedback in the forms of web forms, email messages or simply the 'clicking' patterns, which the tourism marketer can use to development new products or tailor-make existing products to suit the needs of particular consumer(s). In this sense, the Internet has accelerated a shift in the nature of products from mass produced and tangible to customised and information based.

On the other hand, the self-servicing tourist can not only conduct transactions online and reduce costs of sales for the supplier but also actively participate in the production process itself. Provided with choices, a tourist can now assemble his own product according to the specifications desired. This is especially useful in the production and marketing of package holidays. Tour operators, for example, can offer modular products or services, such as flights, rooms, tours, car hire and performances on their web sites, and allow the user to participate in the development of the specific holiday packages using a menu of options, ie., 'pick and mix" his own package.

As tour operators negotiate with the providers of these separate holiday items and buy in bulk, The economies of scale will enable the operators to offer lower "parts" prices to individual consumers than they buy directly from the different producers of the travel products. At the meantime, since the booking engine is integrated with the product inventory, it is easy for the operator to adjust in real-time the prices of different holiday components in response to their relative popularity and demand patterns. In this way, tour operators can effectively provide the market with low cost and flexible package tours. This is what both marketers and consumers have long dreamed for - high quality products made individually at a unit cost level of mass production -all enabled by the power of the Internet. The Internet also give tourist attractions such as museums and galleries wider format options for electronic presentation and show web collections which are physically impossible to construct. Zoos and aquariums can improve its product offering through 'live" camera links using web sites like whale-watching to show views of animals not in captivity.

Pricing

The role of the Internet in pricing is based on its ability in processing and exchanging large amount of data instantaneously with a great number of people. This information processing capacity enables a company to analyze relevant pricing data effectively and quickly. The information exchange capacity enables firms to set and change prices in real time and also facilitates online bidding and flexible pricing. Both of these qualities of the Net are extremely useful in tourism marketing. In Internet marketing, the potential for price discrimination is diminished given the enhanced capability of consumers to identity the least expensive source, regardless of supplier or location. The skilled consumer could have the "perfect knowledge" of market prices, which could facilitate the realization, to certain extent, of 'perfection competition" at the national and global markets.

This will lead to the increasing standardisation of prices across companies or even borders, especially for the undifferentiated products such as airline seats, beach holidays and city breaks. Other applications of pricing on the Web including bidding and flexible pricing - many web-based businesses allow customers to bid for products on their sites. Customers commit to the sale if the price is agreed upon. The bidding locks in customers to the sale and the committed price. This is a flexible pricing strategy where the buying capacity of the customer reflects in the eventual price.

Airlines could sell seats on over-demanded flights or routes through online bidding to the highest bidders to generate extra revenue. Tour operators may use online bidding in a different manner to market special holidays the demand for which may be extremely difficult to estimate in advance. For example, a tour operator can put on its web site the details of a package holiday to the moon and the total cost for a group, say 50 travellers, the more people bid the lower the price for each traveller. This way of pricing could well enhance the operator's image and profitability, as it is both an innovative marketing and sound financial approach.

Place

The uniqueness of the Internet as a means of distribution is based on the fact that it exists in "cyberspace" thus physical phenomena such as location and distance are less significant or even irrelevant. For the producer, the Web enables it to have direct links with consumers at a low cost therefore provides it with the opportunity of "disintermediation". For the retailer, the Web threatens its livelihood and changes its critical success factor from location, location, location to access, access, access. For the wholesaler, web-based business means it can bypass retailers while at the same time risk being bypassed by the producers. The foremost role of the Web in tourism distribution is the direct electronic reservation and transactions between tourism product supplier and consumers.

Direct marketing is the name of the game on the Internet, offering both consumers and marketers greater control and lower potential costs of access due to the conveniences of the Net. Because direct channels may be producer-direct or intermediary-direct, the potential for channel conflict will be magnified. In order to assuage channel conflict and price competition between direct-sellers and retailers, both producers and intermediaries will have to develop augmented product features and unique benefits. For example, direct online booking of airline tickets often carries special benefits not available from travel agents, such as extra frequent-flyer miles; while purchasing an airline ticket from an online travel agency may also benefit from such services as hotel reservations and travel insurance.

The Web offers the airlines even greater opportunities in streamlining and shortening the distribution channel. The no-frills or low-cost airlines emerged in the last few years are already heavily relying on the Web to distribute flight tickets directly to customers. The major global airlines have also started to believe that the Internet offers a unique opportunity to drive down costs and restore profitability to the sector which is troubled with financial losses across the globe. For tour operators, the potential disintermediation has a dual effect. On the one hand, they can be bypassed by the producer as airlines and hotels that directly sell their products to the travel agencies and consumers; on the other, tour operators could benefit from its own direct sell operation by eliminating the travel retailers.

It is hard to estimate the full impacts of the two. But one thing is sure to say that the tour operators, more than travel agencies, have a future in the Internet era. This is based on the understanding that tour operators are not purely intermediaries as they do perform some production function in assembling the various parts of tourism products into a marketable package. Through this value-creating activities, tour operators can provide convenience and better value for consumers, by passing on to them some cost savings gained through bulk buying the separate components of the package, than they would otherwise get from the individual tourist product providers. The major tour operators (in the UK) are also 'backward" integrated and have their own charter airlines thus major schedule airlines' direct selling is not much as a threat to them as to travel agents.

Promotion

Arguably, the component of the marketing mix being most

quickly transformed as a result of Internet usage is promotion. The Internet provides a labour-efficient and cost-effective way of distributing information almost instantaneously to millions of potential clients in the global markets. Internet promotion combines mass media's reach with the personalization inherent in two-way dialogue - previously only possible in personal selling. It can be used for corporate visibility, brand name recognition, advertising, public relations, corporate sponsorship, direct sales, sales promotion, customer support and technical assistance. There are three main issues in the application of the Internet to tourism promotion.

First, present the promotional information on the company's web site. The Web enables more information to be transmitted to (potentially) more people cheaply, instantly and with multimedia effect. The key to achieve these benefits is a well-designed and maintained web site which is attractive, informative and interactive. Through its multimedia capability, a good web site can and should incorporate information as accurate and detailed as brochures or timetables, photos and graphs as glossy as magazine ads, and videos as entertaining as TV commercials. The site can and supply as much promotional information as possible as there is virtually no capacity constraints or advertising space limits on the Web.

By hyper-'inking pages together in an appropriate fashion, the Web marketer can create an ultra-comprehensive brochure to include everything a user wishes to know. For instance, a tourism destination web site may become a 'information mall" which provides the users with all the basic information about it such as the exchange rates, local traditions, weather, what to buy, etc. and, through the hyperlinks to the sites of tourism firms, details of flight schedules, tour prices, park opening times, late offers, and so on. A company web site with email links or even telephone numbers and address will enable users to contact it for further and often more personalised information.

Second, promote the web site itself to increase its exposure and visitation since a company's web site has to compete in the clutter of thousands of other web sites selling similar products and services. This can be achieved through a number of ways. A memorable Internet address to help user locate it on the Web, usually the company or brand name or a catchy word or phrase. Links "from" other web sites, by registering with search engines and online directories and paying relevant sites for click-through links or banners ads, are particularly important if the company's site is not well known. Links 'to" other sites, such as those offer news or entertainment services and those offer complementary products can also make the site more interesting as well as providing more relevant and up-to-date information for the users. Promoting the web site through the traditional media is also important, especially when it was first set up.

Third, use the company's web site as a platform for advertising sites or products of other businesses. Through "banners" and banner linked web pages, a company's web site can also generate revenues by becoming an advertising medium for other organisations. Indeed, the effectiveness of the Web as a medium for advertising has already made online advertising a boom business itself. It also finds that banner advertisements is the predominate type of advertising, accounting for 56%, sponsorships at 27%, interstitials at 4%, email at 2%, and other rounding out the category at 11%. Increased Web advertising will reduce the attractiveness and spending on some traditional forms of promotion such as direct mail, outdoor displays and radio advertising. Fletcher Research predicted that the online advertising spending in the UK would soar from £50 million in 1999 to £625 million by 2004, while expenditures on direct mail could see a 33% fall in the same period.

Current Level Online Travel

The Internet has created great opportunities for tourism marketing. However, the current level of online travel sales is low though most researchers expect it to increase rapidly in the next few years. For example, it was estimated that purchases of travel products represent just 6% of overall Internet sales and 0.5% of all travel and tourism spending. In the US, Jupiter Communications forecasts that online travel bookings will grow from US$2.2 billion in 1998 to US$ 16.6 billion by 2003, representing a market share of total travel sales of 1.7% and 9.6% respectively. In the UK, Thomas Cook predicts that one in five package holidays and 40% of all flights will be sold via the internet or digital television in the next three years. Obviously, the comparative advantages of using the Internet in tourism marketing is compelling but its full potential as a marketing tool will only be realised if a number of well-documented limitations are successfully addressed.

Consumer demand

Consumer demand is the fundamental determinant of all forms of businesses. Whether an industry is initially supply-led or demand-driven, consumers are the key force in deciding the scale, structure, style and speed of its development. The small size of Internet business transactions in the world economy at present is caused to a great extent by insufficient demand, though more limited by consumers' willingness than their ability to shop on the Net.

First, the penetration rate of computer using and Internet connections is still low worldwide. In the main developed countries, about 30-50% of the adult population are Internet users while the global average is about 1-2%. One estimate shows that in 1997, there were 50.2 million web-users, of which 60% were in US and 20% in Europe; the world total web-population in 2001 was predicted to be

174.5 million, the US and Europe account for 54% and 18% respectively. Although people with Internet access tend to be more affluent, better educated and younger than the average consumer, the small number of web-population does reveal that globally it is still a relatively small market. Furthermore not all web-user are frequent users.

Second, the low frequency of web surfing is mainly caused by high access cost, especially in countries outside of North America. In the UK for example, local telephone charges are still metered, though the Internet subscription fees has largely gone from last year. Most consumers find it is an expensive hobby to surf the Web, especially when the search task is complicated by low speed and difficulties in locating the desired information. The main UK Internet service providers (ISPs) have recently launched unmetered packages which will be available from mid-2000. This new development could see a surge in web visitation in the country.

Third, The vast majority of users access web sites for information or entertainment purposes rather than for online shopping. Among the Net resources, email is the most frequently used, news and sports sites attract more visitors than commercial sites, and sex and MP3 are for many years the most searched key words. Although Internet transactions offer the potential benefits of convenience and cost savings, due to factors discussed later, consumers still believe traditional shopping methods are more reliable and sometimes more economical. A recent survey of 50,000 Internet users in the UK show that 80% used the Web to access email while less than a third had bought online.

Fourth, concerns over privacy, information abuse, web crime, payment security and undelivery or late delivery, are often cited as the main inhibitor to online shopping. There is a lot of trust involved in online shopping. A web users has to trust that he receives the product he orders as well as trust its quality to be as described. He also wants to be sure that his private information such as address and credit card numbers is handled sensitively. However, there is at present no special legal provision to protect consumers' interest in web transactions and according to a Consumers International survey: 6% of the items ordered took more than a month to arrive and at least 8% never did; many sites did not give clear information about delivery charges; only 13% of sites promised that they would not sell customers' personal information on to a third party; and only 53% of the companies had a policy on returning goods.

Finally, consumers' anxiety over safety and security in online shopping is further exacerbated by frequent media reports about web security breaches and frauds, and insufficient knowledge of the matter itself. Most of the security worries are caused by people who are not sufficiently aware of the possible protection that exists. Although the Web is generally considered to be user friendly and even 'foolproof", a user without the proper IT knowledge and skills will certainly encounter more problems and feel less confident in conducting web-based transactions.

Technological factors

Many of the current constraints and problems of conducting web-based business are caused by the Web technology itself. 'Web technologies consist of the hardware, software and networks that enable individuals and organisations to connect with and interact with the World Wide Web. Hardware consists of the client terminals, the server, the gateway, the router, and hubs. The software consists of operating and application software, including the browsers and application software on the client side, database servers, web servers and other application servers on the server side, and network operating systems and managers on the network side. The networks consist of cables, either leased or proprietary, and message carrier services". The main causes for concern over the ability of the Web in implementing c-commerce are as follows:

The Web's slow speed, often dubbed as the 'world wide wait", slows down the growth of the web-based businesses as users are often not prepared to wait for too long to see the information appears on the screen. The slowness of the Web is a combined results of three factors: the increasing number of Internet users, the increasing frequency of use, and the increasing richness of the information being transferred over the Internet. Technology will not reduce these growing demands on the Web, on the contrary, technology will constantly expand the Web's capacity for accommodate and even stimulate the increasing demand.

Functionally, the Internet is close to fully operational for commercial purposes. The main remaining impediment to maximum use of the Internet for c-commerce is the concerns for information security. The securing of information includes the protection of: (1) confidentiality - providing confidentiality in the transmission of data; (2) authentication -proving the identification of the individuals both transmitting and receiving the data; certifying that all parties to a transaction are indeed who they claim to be; and (3) non-repudiation - providing proof that the transaction actually took place, establishing an irrefutable time stamp on the sending and receiving of the message. In particular, there is an urgent need for an integrated financial transaction system that is suitable for an open electronic marketplace such as the Internet. How the consumer will pay for goods and services and how the provider will receive the payment securely over the Internet are issues which are being seen as some of the most important success factors for Internet commerce.

Furthermore, the 'unorganised" nature of the Web, makes it difficult to locate the information users desired. The Web offers an uncontrolled and vast universe of information: there are now about 5 million web sites with some 1 billion web pages. However, there is no overriding structure and control over information, no single entry point to the Web, and no centralized directory of content. Although the development of search engines and online directories has made finding information somewhat simpler, it i~ still easy to get distracted or lost during a search and much precious time can be wasted in gathering information. Ironically, this may negate the productivity benefits that derived from its use.

Organisational factors

The low level of web-based business is also attributable to the failure of business organisations in implementing the Web technologies in operation and marketing. Most business leaders did not realise the potential impacts of the Web on commerce until very recently (some still do not). A survey of US hotel managers found that they believe the Internet will 'someday" become an effective marketing and communication tool but not at the present time. Ironically, respondents with greater exposure to the Net rated its present usefulness lower than those with no net experience. On the other hand, those same experienced users gave the Net's future prospects a much higher rating than the inexperienced respondents.

Many companies, even with recognition of the advantages of the Internet in marketing, failed to exploit its full potential due to the lack of management commitment, investment capital and the qualified technical and managerial personnel. This is particularly the case for small tourism businesses. In the UK for example, travel agents are not using the Internet to provide better service to customers because of perceived investment and access costs and fear of new technology. Sabre (UK) recently discovered that fewer than half of its agency customers had an email address. On the other hand, some large travel corporations failed to develop web-based operations wholeheartedly due to both complacency about their market leader positions and the vested interest in their highly vertically integrated business structure.

The top three tour operators in the UK - Thomson, Airtours and First Choice - for instance, did not have a formal Internet strategy until March 2000. They probably overlooked the potential of the new Internet start-ups since the Net-commerce had a slow start and the travel web sites were mainly selling airline seats instead of package tours. The major tour operators were also concerned with the impacts of web-based operation on their own travel agent chains because the "disintermediation" in travel distribution saves operator side cost at the expense of losing businesses at the agency side.

As a result, not all tourism companies are on the Web. When they are on the Web, most of their web sites are PR or promotion sites that provide merely the companies a presence on the Net or little more than advertisements for their products and services. With the few comprehensive sales and transactions web sites, users were often asked to phone an operator or offered a brochure in the post. Just a fifth of the UK's top 40 tour operators have a real-time booking facility on their Internet sites. A recent survey also shows that 62% of the travel companies which have facilities to sell via the Web or email have less than 1% of its total business is conducted through online booking.

Even when web sites are fully operational in real-time transactions, such as many airlines owned sites, they often offer limited choice. Consumers increasingly want to use the web, and they want the convenience to see all the options in one place, no matter which airlines or tour operator is involved. However, most of the travel products on sale over the Net are stored at various web sites owned and operated by individual companies, such as airlines, tour operators, travel agencies and ferry companies. Another problem is that the Web does not always offer the lowest prices compared with the traditional distribution outlets. Research by Express Money shows that booking holidays and flights through the Internet is not cheaper and traditional, low-cost outlets offer lower prices for several popular destinations.

This is particularly the case for airlines as where a single flight could have over 50 different fares, the cheapest fares are usually given to flight-brokers or consolidators. Since most web users consider 'price" as the most important factor in buying an airline ticket, they will certainly be discouraged from booking directly on the Web when they realise that the traditional agents offer better deals.

Governmental Factors

The nature of the Internet enables no one to control its structure and content, while as a recent phenomenon, laws and standards are yet to be developed and adopted to facilitate and regulate its commercial use. Some of the problems highlighted above are partly attributable to or greatly escalated by the lack of effective government involvement in promoting, facilitating and regulating e-commerce on the Internet. Governments across the world have been slow in realising the potential of the Internet for economic growth and even slower in providing the necessary regulatory framework appropriate for conducting Net-based business.

Although existing business laws and regulations are applicable to e-commerce, the particular nature of Internet-based business does requires special treatment, especially in the areas of security, fraud, sabotage, and data and consumer protection. Without the confidence and trust of those participating in the process, it will be impossible to achieve sustainable growth in e-commerce. However, censoring indecent and potentially criminal material on the Internet were often the main reasons chosen for regulation.

In the UK, one of the advanced Net-economies, the Government put forward a draft Electronic Communications bill last year which deals with a wide range of issues central to the healthy development of e-commerce, including consumer protection, information security, authentication and digital signatures, confidentiality, encryption, taxation issues, intellectual property rights, technical standards, illegal content and so on. The problem is, the bill remains to be a draft bill until the Parliament passes it through a lengthy process that could last for years.

As the Internet is a global computer network and e-commerce is essentially global business, the establishment of international standards and legal provisions for its smooth function is also critical. International bodies like the Organisation for Economic Cooperation and Development (OECD) and the European Union (EU) started to address some of the key issues in e-commerce from 1998, such as building trust in electronic commerce by ensuring the security and privacy of information and the protection of consumers; establishing ground rules for electronic transactions; and enhancing the information infrastructure through common interoperable standards, and access to open networks. However, progress is lamentably slow. It appears that each country will have to create their own Internet acceptable use policies, and figure out how to enforce them. Until then, the Internet will be a lawless frontier where anarchy and vigilantism are alive and well.

Legislation is of fundamental importance, but legal provisions only mark the boundary of unacceptable business practices and protect the consumer by redressing any illegal treatment. Consumers want to buy from companies that are not only law-abiding but more importantly are reliable and offer quality and value. Nevertheless, it is extremely difficult, if not impossible, to judge a company by its web site. Therefore, other (non-legal) measures must also be taken to boost consumer confidence in online shopping. The UK Government is trying to promote the ideas of 'e-hallmarks" which will guarantee that its users are legitimate traders offering assurances on security of payments and communications and giving accurate information on goods, prices and a returns policy.

A new body -TrustUK - will be set up to accredit c-commerce codes and there are plans to market the c-hallmark internationally. However, many business organisations oppose the idea, wanting instead to rely on self-regulation without government intervention. For example, ABTA aims to clamp down on Internet sales by creating regulations for online travel transactions. It plans to publish a single revised code of conduct for agents and operators in May 2000, with a new section on Internet sales. It will require members to have a secure payment system if using the Internet to take bookings, and to observe the same ABTA rules as for other types of advertising.

The government can also play an active role in e-commerce by providing the necessary infrastructure for conducting Internet business. After all, the Internet was first started by Government - the US Department of Defence - in 1969 as ARPANet and only became commercialised in 1993. Uncertainty in many countries with regard to policies for investment, ownership, technology selection and general public access to the Internet has restricted the development of Net-based business and the penetration of Internet itself. Especially in the developing world, the huge investment required to establish the network and to make full use of it is out of reach of many businesses. In such circumstances, government could provide start-up funding for small companies. The UK government is also trying to close the gap between technology haves and have-nots and has launched an initiative to make computers available to low-income families for as little as £5 a month.

Development of Hospitality Industry through Email Marketing

The marketing power of the Internet in terms of reach and frequency. Nowhere is this better illustrated than through email marketing. Following the lead of the airlines, many hospitality managers are evaluating email marketing for its low cost, rapid dissemination, and measurability. As many marketers have demonstrated, a well-executed email strategy can produce results. It can strengthen existing market share while at the same time reach new markets to boost revenues, particularly online-generated revenues.

Powerful Marketing Tool

Email marketing is a crucial component of the hotel eMarketing and online distribution strategy. The shift toward online purchasing suggests that the website is becoming a key point of entry to establish interactive relationship with your customers and capture client email profiles. Over 192 million North Americans are active Internet users (Nielsen) and 37 million of them have already purchased travel online. The Internet offers a vast, interactive, content-rich media and most importantly, a growing distribution channel for the hospitality market.

Email gets the most attention of any hospitality eMarketing effort because intuitively it makes sense—since email can create direct revenue opportunities with past, present, and future customers. Email marketing increases revenue opportunities throughout each customer's purchasing life cycle. The reason this is effective is because a total email marketing strategy addresses the entire buying process from initial email capture to message evaluation and everything in between including copy creation, type of messaging, follow-up, and vendor partnership, all components of a comprehensive communications strategy Once the strategy is built, an effective email campaign serves as a powerful sales force and marketing channel.

Why a total email marketing strategy in hospitality makes competitive sense:

— Serves both as direct-response vehicle and branding tool
— Creates personalized interactive relationships with customers
— Targets and entices recipients with relevant promotions
— Plants seed in the minds of recipients regarding future travel plans
— Serves as a tool to move distressed inventory
— Functions as a sales force – tens of thousands reached in seconds
— Recruits and retains customers, new and old
— Least expensive form of active marketing available

Use of Email

Everyone uses email. We read, forward, file, and print email. We send email to friends, family, and clients. Furthermore, almost everybody has at one time or another actively signed up to receive travel related information from a travel supplier or third-party collection service. Travel is a sought after product and a top information category chosen by most Internet users.

By category, travel related email marketing retains a loyal audience, especially if it offers the recipient value, accurate communication, relevance, and familiarity. Forrester Research points out that on average, only 5 percent of recipients have ever unsubscribed from any travel related list. Indeed, some travel-related email campaigns report response rates as high as 25%. Consumers want to learn about travel specials and promotions. Even travel agents serve as a viable audience as they too seek bookable opportunities.

Thanks to technology and the law, filtering agents and anti-spam laws have begun reigning-in annoying junk email. Filtering products such as Spamex and Spamcop, which cost less than $30 off the shelf, delete messages sent by anonymous senders to group lists and can filter by key words in the message itself. The laws are getting tougher. Third-party email messaging vendors, also called service bureaus, and marketers are increasingly wary of these laws and are leading the charge to protect the privacy and protection of email recipients.

Permission-based Email Marketing

Permission-based email marketing is the second-generation email approach that goes well beyond guerilla email marketing, known as email spam. A permission-based customer list is one in which you asked the customer permission to enter personal information voluntarily including an email address for the purpose of marketing, i.e. you obtain "permission" to send promotional emails. Opt-in or opt-out options enable the user to sign up or be removed from a marketing list. Growth in permission-based, 100% opt-in, opt-out practices consistently cleanse the customer lists to produce the most robust client lists possible. Once a firm starts an email collection process, it should include these features resulting in email that will be opened and read time and again without concern of violating email privacy norms.

Precision e-mail marketing is the next, third generation email approach that dynamically "reads" customer profiles, purchasing habits and history to create highly personalized emails. Over the past year airlines have used this type of marketing extensively to promote special offers in order to sell seats. Actually, permission based email and precision email marketing have become the airlines' preferred marketing tool. It is cheap and it works. For example, precision e-mail marketing has generated up to a fivefold increase in response rates and tenfold lower conversion costs than direct mail.

Make Sense

— *Low cost*: Email is relatively inexpensive, pennies per email compared to $1 to $3 or more per direct mail.

— *Reach*: Almost instant outreach to an expansive client base, one email blast can be equivalent to thousands of sales calls.

— *Protects brand integrity*: Enables promotion of the latest specials on a one-to-one basis to a pre-selected audience without announcing to the world the latest discounts.

— *Personalization*: The recipient thinks this is a personalized invitation at a preferred customer rate.

— *Instant gratification*: People are at their computers most of the day and can receive, respond, forward, and print email almost immediately.

— *Rich Media*: Email marketing comes in various styles: text, e-Newsletters, HTML messages like a postcard or survey. The hotel gets its message across with sound, color, animation, video, whatever is most appropriate.

— *Results*: Outcomes based, from knowing who opened the message, clicked on which links, how much time spent viewing each page, completed a transaction, or forwarded the email.

Distressed Inventory

Group cancellations and overestimations can make empty rooms the biggest competitor. It is well-known that the September 11th tragedy left hotels scrambling for solutions. Using email to move distressed inventory is an effective, practical option. With a well-executed message matched with a robust customer list, an email campaign can begin producing revenues within 24 hours without weakening brand integrity. The challenge is in collecting the right data and stratifying the data list to meet campaign objectives.

Customers Email Marketing

This is an important question. There are three main groups of email audiences: consumers (leisure or business), travel intermediaries (travel agents, wholesalers) and corporate clients. If a significant percentage of reservations come from transient business travelers, or from overseas tour operators, build campaigns that focus on these client segments.

Consumer Email Marketing

Hoteliers can either buy a broadcast to a permission-based consumer email list from any number of third-party vendors or create their own "home-grown" email capture strategy, or do both. Renting from a third-party is an efficient short-term strategy. It creates an immediate audience and serves as a supplement to your own customer email database. Long-term, starting immediately, it is important to build an in-house customer database as part of a total email strategy. It is critical to capture client data at the property-level for the purpose of creating highly relevant, targeted email marketing campaigns.

Hoteliers are in a unique position to build a robust list from existing customers. Using a list built from existing customers, the conversion rates can be ten times greater than any standalone rented mailing list because the targeted group already knows and has experienced the product first-hand. In addition, the hotel can stratify the customer list by specific characteristics, communicate and offer value in the message, and send targeted and relevant mailings frequently to the intended audience, an audience that even anticipates these messages announcing hotel specials.

Hoteliers should carefully consider how large and comprehensive a customer list would be from a home grown collection strategy. Anyone who has stayed, inquired, or visited the property, visited the hotel website, or spoken to a receptionist by phone or in person qualifies.

An organically grown database of customers can exceed the value of any customer list worth renting.

Reasons for building a homegrown customer list:

— Represents an existing client base

— Serves as a tool to access greater audiences, i.e. friends, family, colleagues

— Builds retention and overall loyalty

— Ownership of the database

— Low cost

Any perceivable point of contact with customers: in the reservations process, on the website, through convention attendee lists, holiday parties, weddings, special events, at the front desk from walk-in customers, phone inquiries, groups and tour operators, travel agents and vendors.

Capture Email on the Hotel Website

If so, that website might draw 10,000 visitors per month, if optimized for the search engines. A conservative look to book ratio of 20:1 yields 500 transactions per month. Consider another 5% will sign up for promotions but not book producing, another 500 registrations. The total number annualized from the website could result in an estimated 12,000 new client profiles added to the database.

How does a hotel compare to today's average where 8%-10% of all revenues in hospitality are generated from the Internet? It is estimated that four years from now the Internet will contribute over 18% of all hotel bookings. Hoteliers are beginning to like what they see as online distribution cuts costs, attracts affluent customers and lessens the dependency on more traditional and expensive distribution channels. Hotels must employ new strategies to take advantage of these opportunities to capture this Internet market.

Travel Agent Email Marketing

Travel agents that use the Internet and email are exactly the travel agents hoteliers must reach. These agents are likely to visit hotel websites, book online, and even boast hotel web-only promotions in their own marketing efforts to preferred clients. Research from the most respected travel organizations, such as ARC, ASTA, IATA and Plog Research, as well as leading travel industry trade publications shows that:

— 96 percent of agents send and receive e-mail

— 79 percent of agents receive e-mail travel requests from clients

— 54 percent of agents e-mail clients with special offers or incentives

Collecting Right Data

Collecting the right information is essential to not confuse long-term marketing plans. For example, in selling automobiles, single males and females have their own particular tastes and needs as do families and seniors. By asking the right set of questions on the website and at the front desk, the dealer can stratify his database to reach discrete audiences with the appropriate set of messages. It is essential to consider which audiences the hotel wants to reach and with what types of messages.

Based on the type of hotel and other variables, one can begin to get an idea of what data is important to build a customer database. It is critical to avoid the 9-deadly sins of email marketing and not appear anxious or aggressive when collecting client information. The hotel must collect with sensitivity resulting in a process that runs on autopilot whether it's online or through your reservation desk. Start collecting the data!

It is important to follow the path of the customer! Exploit every point of entry from the reception desk and corporate sales office, to the reservation operator and website. Create an environment suitable for data collection; client profiles from call-ins, walk-ins, or online lookers regardless if they are patrons, travel agents, or others. At the same time, a central repository will be helpful to avoid repeat inquiries from the same customers. The hotels should always seek permission. It's been shown that if a hotel asks permission and clearly demonstrates how one can opt-in or out easily and conveniently, chances are the user will sign up and remain a loyal recipient of hotel emails. Such collection tactics include:

— Sign our "Guest Book"
— Announce a drawing
— Offer a promotion or special discount
— Refer a friend
— Follow up e-Questionnaire
— eSurvey

Store Data

Outsourcing the technology support for email marketing makes complete sense. In 2001, an estimated 72% of all email campaigns were outsourced. Third-party vendors or "service bureaus" are inexpensive and this is their core competency. These vendors specialize in email messaging including email capture, hosting, managing, stratifying, blasting, and reporting outcomes of the campaign.

There are a plethora of third-party vendors ready to serve technology needs and act as guardian of the data. These low cost highly competitive ASP technologists want hotel business and can provide, at minimal cost, features and formats to capture, create, and blast a campaign. Some vendors offer templates to help design an eNewsletter while others support Macro Media for Flash. Hotels should understand the level of customer service each vendor offers. Of course, stick to your budget.

Not surprisingly some online booking technology vendors offer email collection and messaging management. A reputable service bureau adheres to the strictest rules permitted by law and will maintain client information in a secure environment. They will not rent or barter information to outsiders. However, hoteliers should seek advice on vendor selection, review of campaign, and vendor agreement.

Email Campaign

There are a number of guides to email marketing, starting with the marketing objectives. A quality email campaign delivers comfortable, interesting content, and offers value in the form of premiums, discounts, or specials. Whenever possible, the hotel should avoid the hard sell, be brief and to the point and never overstate the message. Today's browsers support viewing many forms of inviting eNewsletters. Information delivered in this fashion reinforces the hotel brand—its logo and colors—and organizes the delivery of content so that a quick glance may be all that's necessary to draw the user to link to a hotel website and book now. Other suggestions include the need to clearly identify the hotel and intent in the subject line and property insignia. In addition, subject line must be relevant and personalized, if possible.

9

Directions for Hotel Managers

The central components of direction are mission, vision, business definition, and values. Top managers are charged with the responsibility of providing long-term direction for their organizations, while at the same time balancing the competing interests of key stakeholders. One of the critical errors that some organizations make is that they do not know who they are, how they got to where they are, or where they are going. They suffer an "identity crisis". There are no widely accepted guidelines managers use to provide strategic direction.

Some companies have adopted formal statements for each of these areas. However, regardless of the medium of communication, high-performing companies tend to create an organizational identity that is understood by both internal and external stakeholders. On the inside, a well-established organizational identity can provide guidance to managers at all levels as they make strategic decisions.

In addition, communicating strategic direction to external stakeholders can increase their understanding of the motives of the organization, and it may also facilitate the creation of inter organisational relationships, since potential partners have a greater ability to judge the existence of common goals. One corporate president stated that "his company's mission statement has helped create a 'partnering attitude' instead of an adversarial relationship" between his company and its customers. Both internal and external stakeholders influence strategic direction. The amount of influence stakeholders have is proportional to their economic, political, and formal (legal or contractual) power. The broad environment is also influential.

For example, an organization usually tries to establish a value system that is consistent with what society expects, or at least appears to be consistent. Also, economic, technical, and political/legal realities influence the selection of business areas in which to compete. Strategic direction forms the foundation from which plans of action are developed. Actions include the firm's competitive strategies, implementation strategies, control systems, and the way internal and external stakeholders and stakeholder relationships are managed. Organizational actions lead to particular outcomes, such as market successes or failures, and to financial performance, which includes sales growth.

Also, stakeholders will respond to the actions of organizations in a variety of ways. For instance, customers could be pleased with the services of an organization, or they could be angry and file a lawsuit against the company. Employees could be happy, or they could strike. Government regulators could be cooperative, or they could interfere with operations through fines and penalties. These outcomes translate into feedback that the organization can use to adjust strategic direction, actions, or both direction and actions. Feedback becomes a part of the organization's history. History can potentially assist strategic planning processes, since organizations can learn from past successes and failures.

Unfortunately, history can also be a weakness that stands in the way of forward progress. Past successes sometimes create strong structural inertia, the term for forces at work to maintain the status quo. These forces can include systems, structures, processes, culture, sunk costs, internal politics, and barriers to entry and exit. Anything that favours the "status quo" has the potential to cause inertia. Inertia is stronger when an organization has been successful in the past because managers believe that past success will translate into future success, regardless of early warning signals to the contrary. Inertia, then, is another potential threat to the survival and prosperity of an organization.

Structural inertia is related to human nature. Most humans desire a certain amount of predictability in their work. In other words, they have learned to cope with their organizational environment-they are comfortable. They may also fear that changes will reduce their own power or position in the organization or that they will no longer be considered competent. If the forces favouring inertia are strong and if the organization has been successful in the past, people will be highly resistant to any major shift in missions or strategies. Inertia based on past successes was one of the main reasons for the decline of the railroads as a form of passenger transportation. They continued to pursue the same strategies until it was simply too late.

An organization's mission statement provides an important vehicle for communicating ideals and a sense of direction and purpose to internal and external stakeholders. It can inspire employees and managers. It can also help guide organizational managers in resource-allocation decisions. Clearly, not all "opportunities" that organizations face will be compatible with their missions. If used properly, an organization's mission should provide a screen for evaluating opportunities and proposals. Sometimes students of strategic management confuse the terms mission and vision. In general, a mission is what the organization is and its reason for existing, whereas a vision is a forward-looking view of what the organization wants to become.

Mission Statements

Statements about the values of an organization. As long as

an organization understands what it is, what it values, and where it is going, then it has a well-defined strategic direction. The particular labels are not as important as making sure that all aspects of strategic direction are included. Following is one example of how a company chose its path:

One hotel general manager's direction-setting experience shows that sometimes the vision emerges in discussions with the senior management staff but is not written down initially. According to the general manager of a Hilton-branded property who crafted a vision for his hotel, it was a change in thinking first and foremost. "We were going to become the best corporate hotel positioned at the top end, but I approached this vision by doing three things, living my values, constantly talking about our vision, and modelling the vision every day. The plan was shockingly devoid of systems or procedures. I felt it and was deeply into it. The hotel needed an identity in the minds of the employees, and my job was to bring a deep belief in what this hotel could become to these people. My agenda? Focus and model, focus and model. I just did what seemed right at the time. "

It was not until almost six years later when the general manager was executive vice president of the hotel group, a company that owned and managed hotels branded with a variety of different midpriced and upper-priced hotel franchisers, that he created a formal vision of what the hotel aspired to become. After considerable thought he arrived at the simple statement, "the friendliest place to visit. "As organizations are first established, their mission may be as simple as "Provide lowcost lodging to highway travezlers while generating a profit for the owner. " The mission is often informal and is seldom written down. But notice that even in its simplest form, this mission encompasses a purpose, a brief definition of the business, and two important stakeholders, the owner and the customer.

Most businesses begin with a mission that is just as simple as the example given. The mission is an extension of the entrepreneur or entrepreneurs who form the organization. As companies succeed in their business environments, opportunities arise that allow the firm to grow in revenues and number of employees, and encourage it to expand into new product and market areas. The original mission may seem too restrictive. At this point, the organization will probably begin to pay more attention to previously overlooked or neglected stakeholders.

For example, the company may increase employee benefits (employees), hire additional tax specialists (government), designate a public-relations officer (society), attempt to negotiate better discounts with suppliers (suppliers), or increase borrowing to help sustain growth (financial intermediaries). In addition, the firm will certainly pay more attention to the actions and reactions of competitors. These stakeholders and forces in the broad environment then become forces that are considered as the organization adjusts or enlarges its mission. At some point in the growth of an organization, planning processes are formalized. This may be the first time that a mission statement is put into words.

Articulating a mission forces top managers to come to terms with some key issues regarding the current direction of the firm and its future. A well-written mission statement can be an excellent tool for conveying the meaning and intent of an organization to its internal and external stakeholders. A mission statement can also be an effective way to communicate to important stakeholders such as shareholders, customers, and employees that the company is aware there is a problem and is trying to fix it. This is important during a turnaround. The huge North American retailer Sears experienced major setbacks in recent years, including market-share erosion in retailing and loss of the market-leadership position to Wal-Mart. Sears' mission statement reflects awareness of difficulties and the outline of a plan for fixing them:

Sears is a company on the move. Our destination is clear. We're pursuing ways to generate profitable growth. We're striving to become more relevant to our customers. We're learning to celebrate our diversity, work together and perform with urgency. And we're establishing new benchmarks for productivity and continuous improvement. By turning individual success stories into models we can replicate across the organization, we can become the destination of choice for customers, employees and investors. Unfortunately, in many organizations the process of developing a written mission statement has deteriorated into an exercise in slogan writing. Managers often worry more about writing a catchy, short phrase that can be printed on a business card than about managing with purpose.

For an organization's mission to be a management tool, it must be grounded in the realities of the business. One of the first steps in creating a clear sense of mission is to fully understand the nature of the business in which the organization participates. This first step, business definition discussed below.

Business

One of the most vital questions management can ask is "Who are we?" A clear business definition is the starting point of all strategic planning and management. It provides a framework for evaluating the effects of planned change and for planning the steps needed to move the organization forward. When defining the business, the question "What is our business?" should be answered from three perspectives:

1. Who is being satisfied?
2. What is being satisfied?

3. How are customer needs satisfied?

The first question refers to the markets that an organization serves, the second question deals with the specific functions provided to the customers identified in question 1, and the third question refers to the capabilities and technologies the firm uses to provide the functions identified in question 2. This approach is, admittedly, marketing oriented. Its greatest strength is that it focuses on the customer, an important external stakeholder for most firms. Candlewood Hotel Company defines its business as follows:

Candlewood Hotel Company, Inc. owns, operates, franchises and manages business travel hotels. The Company's hotel properties cater to mid-market and upscale business and personal travellers seeking multiple night stays. While defining a business is helpful in communicating to internal and external stakeholders what the organization is all about, the business definition should not constrain strategic choice. In other words, it is an excellent tool for identifying where a company is, but it should not be used to determine where the company should go in the future. Peter Drucker suggested that the business-definition question should be stated not only as "What is our business?" but also as "What will it be?" and "What should it be?" The second question refers to the direction that the firm is heading at the current time.

In other words, where will the business end up if it continues in its current course? The third question, "What should it be?" allows for modifications to the existing strategy to move the company in an appropriate direction. Organizations that struggle to come to grips with those two questions are forced to look forward in time and to think about a vision for the future. Gary Hamel suggests that rather than determine the future direction of an organization based on what it does, the organization should think in terms of what it knows and the resources it owns. In other words, a company should determine future direction based on its resources and capabilities. As organizations become involved in businesses outside of their current operations, they are increasing what is referred to as their scope. In other words, the scope of an organization is the breadth of its activities both within a market and across markets. Marriott has stated its intent to broaden its business definition to include related markets. Marriott's mission statement, in part, reads:

Marriott International expects to create significant shareholder value by aggressively growing its existing businesses, and identifying related opportunities which leverage our core skills and can be developed into major new businesses. Delta Air Lines, like many airlines, has adhered to a narrow business definition. Instead of venturing into new areas, in 1986 Delta acquired Western Airlines. This move allowed Delta to greatly increase its western U. S. route coverage and establish an international presence, thus expanding the geographic size of its markets.

However, the type of customer served, function, service, and technologies remained the same. Delta and many other airlines are almost entirely dependent on one business. When the industry experiences downturns and shocks, they have no other businesses to offset losses. This became evident in 2001 when the terrorist attacks in the United States and the associated downturn in demand for air travel led to losses that the airlines could not sustain. When it looked as if many U. S. airlines would go out of business, the federal government provided a multibillion-dollar bailout. On the other hand, Virgin Atlantic Airways is a part of a highly diversified group:

Led by adventurous founder, chairman, and owner Sir Richard Branson, Virgin Group gets around. The group's travel operations, led by 51 percent-owned Virgin Atlantic Airways, are among its biggest breadwinners. Virgin Atlantic is complemented by its pan-European and Australian low-fare cousins, Virgin Express and Virgin Blue.

Virgin Group also operates two UK rail franchises and sells tour packages. The group's Virgin Megastores sell music, videos, and computer games. Other Virgin Group operations include balloon flights, beverages, bridal stores, cosmetics, financial services, health clubs, Internet services, mobile phone services, publishing, and a record label. Virgin's business definition is at the opposite extreme from many lodging, restaurant, and airline companies that tend to focus on only one type of business.

While such high levels of diversity typically are hard to manage, they do provide a cushion against shocks in particular businesses. For now, it is sufficient to say that the execution of a corporate-level strategy results in a particular business definition. For example, if a corporate-level strategy includes increased involvement in particular businesses or business segments, the business definition will be changed to reflect these changes.

Organizational Vision

An organization with a vision has a definite sense of what it wants to be in the future. The CEO has primary responsibility for creating the organizational vision. The vision of Marriott is "to be the world's leading provider of hospitality services. "Marriott, with nearly 2, 600 properties and 144, 000 associates in sixty-seven countries and territories, is arguably fulfilling that vision. Once it is stated, a vision may be used to focus the efforts of the entire organization. For example, plans, policies, or programs that are inconsistent with the corporate vision may need to be altered or replaced. A well-understood vision can help managers and employees believe that their actions have meaning. Unfortunately, sometimes firms have a vision but it produces no positive results because it is not well understood by members of the organization.

A study was conducted at Cornell's School of Hotel Administration in which students were to make contact with an employee of eighty different lodging companies. Many of these contacts were with reservation agents, the point of first contact with the company for many guests. For the majority of the companies multiple contacts were made as a better indication of actual knowledge possessed by employees. Students asked their contact if they knew the vision of the company. Without embarrassing any one lodging company. Of those contacted, 28 percent knew the vision, 3 percent looked it up, 68 percent did not know the vision, and 1 percent provided a rude response.

First, it is possible that many of these firms did not have a vision. Second, those firms that had one were not communicating it very well. Either of these situations results in the same problem. The people who are making contact with guests and other stakeholders don't really understand what their companies are trying to become. Sometimes a vision is more of a concept than a specific goal. In other words, it is a vision of what the organization should be like. Such a vision can still be very motivating and can help establish a culture that guides the actions of individuals.

When Michael Snyder saw his son's horse run free without bit or saddle against the picturesque Colorado backdrop of the snow-capped Rocky Mountains, the idea came to him: "What if a guy could run a company that way? What if you had an organization, powerful, all going the same direction with beauty and grace, effortlessly, unbridled, without restraint?" That was ten years ago when Snyder, now president and CEO of Red Robin International, was just a Red Robin franchisee at the head of The Snyder Group Co. He began applying his unbridled philosophy to his franchise restaurants and, now, after two years in charge of the Englewood, Colorado-based casual-dining, family restaurant/burger joint, he applies his theory to corporate units as well.

A philosopher at heart, Snyder runs Red Robin with a fatherly goodwill towards employees and is modest about his role in the success of the $300-plus million restaurant chain. "I try to surround myself with people who share my values, which are honour, integrity, continually seeking knowledge and having fun, and who are smarter than me, " Snyder says. "What I try to do is provide a healthy, productive, profitable, valuing environment for people to continue through life's journey. "Organizational Values A final but equally important aspect of strategic direction is the establishment of organizational values. Values guide organizational decisions and behaviour. Wendy's International Inc., one of the world's largest restaurant-operating and -franchising companies, has a specific statement of values that should drive organizational decisions and operations:

— *Integrity*: We keep our promises. All actions are guided by absolute honesty, fairness and respect for every individual.

— *Leadership*: We lead by example and encourage leadership qualities at all levels. Everyone has a role to play.

— *People Focus*: We believe our people are key to our success. We value all members of our diverse family for their individual contributions and their team achievements.

— *Customer Satisfaction*: Satisfying internal and external customers is the focus of everything we do.

— Continuous Improvement: Continuous improvement is how we think; innovative change provides competitive opportunities.

— Community Involvement: Giving back is our heritage. We actively participate and invest in the communities where we do business.

— *Commitment to Stakeholders*: We serve all stakeholders and, through balancing our responsibilities to all, we maximize value to each of them. Values statements are common throughout the hospitality industry.

Notice that there are some similarities between these value statements, but there are important differences also. These differences are a reflection of the culture and ethics of the company:

Our values serve as the guide for how we treat our customers, our owners, our shareholders and our associates. We aspire to these values to make Starwood a great place to work and do business. We succeed only when we meet and exceed the expectations of our customers, owners and shareholders. We have a passion for excellence and will deliver the highest standards of integrity and fairness. We celebrate the diversity of people, ideas and cultures. We honour the dignity and value of individuals working as a team. We improve the communities in which we work. We encourage innovation, accept accountability and embrace change. We seek knowledge and growth through learning.

We share a sense of urgency, nimbleness and endeavour to have fun too. High-level managers, especially the CEO, have a great deal of influence on the values of the company. The values of Darden Restaurants were articulated by CEO Joe Lee in a letter to shareholders. When a new top manager takes charge, his or her personal values help shape the entire company. Managers who work with the CEO quickly identify his or her value system and communicate it to lower-level managers and employees. The CEO may also discuss organizational values in speeches, news releases, and memos. To the extent that the CEO controls the rewards systems subjectively, managers who make decisions that are consistent with the values of the CEO are likely to be rewarded, thus reinforcing what is expected.

Many of the people who strongly disagree with the new values will voluntarily leave the firm. Or, if their own behaviour pattern is inconsistent with the new rules of the game, they will be "forced out" through poor performance evaluations, missed promotions, or low salary increases. Thus, over a period of time, the example and actions of the CEO are reflected in most of the major decisions that are made by the organization. In spite of the power of the CEO, he or she is not the only determinant of organizational values. The values of an organization are also a reflection of the social groups from which managers and other employees are drawn (which makes global management even more challenging).

These individuals bring a personal value system with them when they are hired. In the hospitality industry, often times the values of a social group are part of the service experience. Disney's Polynesian resort, for example, offers an entire training program, "Magic of Polynesia, " which is designed to facilitate employee understanding and commitment to the authentic vision of Polynesia. The case members and management identified four theme values as part of their discussion of "what makes us Polynesian. "

The values identified as reflecting Polynesian hospitality included

— a sense of Ohano, or sense of family, which describes the way they would like their working relationships to be;

— a sprit of Aloha, which means that the basis of their interactions is their desire to be caring and mindful of others;

— a sense of Kina'olea, the desire to perform all interactions and services in a high-quality way; and

— a sense of Mea Ho'okipa, the desire to be the perfect host by "welcoming and entertaining guests and strangers with unconditional warmth and generosity. "If value changes in society are not voluntarily incorporated into a firm, an employee or manager may "blow a whistle, " which is an attempt to force the organization to cease a behaviour that society finds unacceptable or to incorporate a practice that is in keeping with the new social value.

For example, antidiscrimination lawsuits have prompted many organizations to adopt more stringent equal employment opportunity policies and even affirmative action programs. The values of various social groups are constantly changing. Therefore, strategic managers need to keep abreast of these changes in order to successfully position their firms. This task is especially difficult in global organizations. Stakeholder theory is closely aligned with discussions of values and social responsibility, since one of the principles underlying the theory is that organizations should behave appropriately with regard to a wide range of stakeholder concerns and interests. The increasing incidence of lawsuits against top managers and their companies in recent years provides evidence that many organizations are not satisfying all of their stakeholders' expectations very well.

Social Responsibility

Embedded within the concept of organizational values is the notion of social responsibility. Social responsibility contains four major components:

- economic responsibilities, such as the obligation to be productive and profitable and meet the consumer needs of society;
- a legal responsibility to achieve economic goals within the confines of written law;
- moral obligations to abide by unwritten codes, norms, and values implicitly derived from society; and
- discretionary responsibilities that are volitional or philanthropic in nature.

The old belief, espoused primarily by economists such as Milton Friedman, is that the only valid objective of a corporation is to maximize profits, within the rules of the game (legal restrictions). While it is true that profits are desirable, they are only one outcome of successful corporations. A corporation that becomes too focused on profits is likely to lose the support and cooperation of key stakeholders such as suppliers, activist groups, competitors, society, and the government. In the long run, this sort of strategy may result in problems such as lawsuits, loss of goodwill, and, ultimately, a loss of profits.

One business-ethics expert argued that There is a long-term cost to unethical behaviour that tends to be neglected. That cost is to the trust of the people involved. Companies today-due to increasing global competition and advancing technological complexity-are much more dependent than ever upon the trust of workers, specialists, managers, suppliers, distributors, customers, creditors, owners, local institutions, national governments, venture partners, and international agencies. People in any of those groups who believe that they have been misgoverned by bribes, sickened by emissions, or cheated by products tend, over time, to lose trust in the firm responsible for those actions.

The case of Manville illustrates these points. Nearly fifty years ago, employees and managers of Manville (then Johns-Manville) started to receive information that asbestos inhalation was associated with various forms of lung disease. Manville chose to ignore this information and to suppress research findings. The company even went so far as to conceal chest X-rays from employees in their asbestos operations. When confronted about this tactic, a Manville lawyer was quoted as saying that they would let their employees work until they dropped dead, all in the interest of saving money. Eventually, this neglect of research findings and their own employees led to financial ruin for Manville. Concerning ethical decision making, the approach of many business organizations seems to be to wait until someone complains before actions are taken.

This is the type of attitude that resulted in the savings-and-loan crisis, the Bhopal explosion tragedy in India, and the explosion of the space shuttle Challenger. In each of these situations, the organizations involved could have avoided problems by being more responsive to warning signals from key stakeholders. History has taught us that many human-induced disasters and crises could be avoided if organizations were sensitive to what one or another of their stakeholders is saying.

Enterprises Strategy

One fundamental question an organization should ask in determining its purpose is "What do we stand for?" This question is the critical link between ethics and strategy. Enterprise strategy is the term used to denote the joining of ethical and strategic thinking about the organization. It is the organization's best possible reason for the actions it takes. Consequently, an enterprise strategy is almost always focused on serving particular stakeholder needs. For example, an enterprise strategy can contain statements concerning a desire to maximize stockholder value, satisfy the interests of all or a subset of other stakeholders, or increase social harmony or the common good of society. Some organizations get very specific about how they will deal with stakeholder interests.

Organizational mission statements containing the elements of an enterprise strategy are more likely to be found in high-performing than in low-performing corporations. Enterprise strategy is a natural extension of the ethics of the organization, which are an extension of the values of key managers within the organization. The ethics of a firm are not just a matter of public statements. Ethical decision making is a way of doing business. A company that specifically works to build ethics into its business practice, to develop and implement an enterprise strategy, will have a frame of reference for handling potential ethical problems.

For this reason it is not surprising that a recent study of hospitality executives revealed that ethics and integrity were considered the most important competencies for the success of future leaders in the industry.

Ethical Frames

The pattern of decisions made by organizational managers establishes strategy and creates expectations among other organizational members and external stakeholders. For example, a firm that has specialized in the highest-quality services creates an expectation among customers that all services will be high quality. If the firm chooses to change its strategy to include lower-quality services, it runs the risk that customers will perceive the change as a breach of faith. Similarly, if a company has an established relationship with a customer as its sole source of supply of a particular product, then the customer comes to depend on that company. If the supplier then chooses to drop that product from its product line, what might seem to be a clear-cut business decision takes on an ethical dimension: Can the customer's business survive if the product is dropped? Should other alternatives be considered? What obligation does the supplier have to that customer?

These types of decisions carry an ethical dimension because they go against what some important stakeholders think is right. An ethical dilemma exists when the values of different stakeholders of the organization are in conflict. Although there is no real legal dimension, an issue of trust or good faith is apparent. In addition to decisions that violate stakeholder expectations, there are also ethical dilemmas related to the gray area surrounding legal behaviour: the definitions of what society views as right and wrong.

The values that organizational members bring to their work-the shared values that make up the organizational culture-determine whether the issues of trust, good faith, and obligation are raised when decisions are being deliberated, as well as the degree to which these issues influence the final outcome. In making decisions that deal with ethical issues, it is important to have a frame of reference. Few ethical dilemmas have simple right-or-wrong answers. Instead, they are complex and require balancing the economic and social interests of the organization. The following are five theoretical models that often influence organizational decisions.

Economic theory: Under economic theory, the purpose of a business organization is to maximize profits. Profit maximization will lead to the greatest benefit for the most people. Other than profit maximization, there are no ethical issues in business. Assumptions of profits being evenly distributed is naive. Not all business decisions relate to profit making, and some ways of increasing profits hurt society.

Legal Theory: Laws are a reflection of what society has determined is right and wrong. Compliance with the law ensures ethical behaviour. The social and political processes used to formulate laws are complex and time consuming. Since the processes are subject to manipulation, the laws may not truly reflect the interests of society.

Religion: Everyone should act in accordance with religious teachings. As a model for business decision making, religious values are difficult to apply. There are many different religious beliefs, and there is no consensus on the behaviors that are consistent with the beliefs.

Utilitarian Theory: Utilitarian theory says to focus on the outcome of a decision. Everyone should act in a way that generates the greatest benefits for the largest number of people. Under this model, immoral acts that hurt society or a minority group can be justified if they benefit the majority.

Universalist Theory: Universalist theory says to focus on the intent of the decision. Every person is subject to the same standards. Weigh each decision against the screen.

This model provides no absolutes. What one person believes is acceptable for all in society may be offensive to others.

It is obvious that the five models do not provide absolute guidance on how to handle an ethical dilemma. Instead, they provide a departure point for discussing the implications of decisions. In addition, conflicts sometimes are easier to resolve if the two parties to the conflict understand each other's perspectives. An awareness of different frames of reference is especially important for hospitality firms that participate in foreign environments. For example, Eastern countries tend to be much more utilitarian in their approach to decisions, whereas larger industrialized Western countries tend to give economics a lot of weight. The influence of religion is strong in some Latin countries. These are obviously overgeneralizations that do not always hold true, but the key is not so much to pin down exactly what perspective a decision maker favours, but rather to look at decisions and conflicts from a variety of perspectives and to be aware that the other party to a transaction may not share your frame of reference.

Code of Ethics

Many organizations create a code of ethics in a further effort to communicate the values of the corporation to employees and other stakeholders. Another benefit of a code of ethics is that it allows the firm to clarify to employees what behaviour is considered appropriate. Some codes of ethics set a minimum standard of behaviour by stating that employees are expected to obey all laws. Other organizations make specific statements about values, duties, and obligations to customers, employees, and societies. Clearly, in those cases, the organization expects members to maintain standards of ethical behaviour that transcend minimum legal standards. The code of ethics of the Resort Hotel Association, a provider of insurance services to the hospitality industry, states:

RHA is member driven and managed. As intermediaries between our member resorts and the companies that provide insurance coverage, we recognize that we must be bound by high standards of ethical conduct. Accordingly, it is our responsibility to RHA members:

— To ensure that insurance coverage will be provided by financially stable organizations.

— To ensure that coverages will be specifically designed to meet the needs of resort hotels.

— To provide adequate limits of coverage.

— To ensure that members' insurance claims are resolved in an equitable, timely and effective manner.

— To provide effective loss-control and risk-management services.

— To strive to make the association a superior insurance risk in the commercial marketplace.

— To adhere to the highest professional standards of conduct.

— To present to our members, accurately and honestly, all facts essential to their buying decisions.

— To maintain strict confidentiality of member information.

— To exemplify the best professional standards of this industry.

— To ensure that employees abide by the corporate code of ethics, some companies establish an ethics system, including an audit process to monitor compliance.

Employees should be encouraged to report violations to their supervisors or a designated corporate ethics officer. Some companies allow these reports to be anonymous through use of tollfree numbers to reduce the possibility of retribution against employees for making reports of violations. Sometimes formal systems are not enough to ensure ethical behaviour.

In an award winning article, "The Parable of the Sadhu, " Bowen McCoy, an investment banker with Morgan Stanley, discussed what he thought was the core, underlying problem when an organization handles ethical dilemmas poorly. In his view, people who are part of an organization often do not personalize ethical issues. It is as if the "organization" is responsible, and the individuals are not. Even individuals who see themselves as very ethical will tend to pass through an ethical dilemma without recognizing it as one, or they will view the dilemma as ultimately someone else's problem. For many ethical dilemmas, one person is not physically capable of correcting the problem alone.

When faced with a major crisis, such as finding that a service is dangerous to the customers who purchase it, many organizations do not know what to do. There is no guiding precept, no system of shared values, to unite the company behind a clear understanding of correct behaviour. Although some company members may feel discomfort with the course of action being pursued by the firm, a change in action requires a structured, systematic effort by the entire organization.

According to McCoy: "Some organizations have a value system that transcends the personal values of the managers. Such values, which go beyond profitability, are usually revealed when the organization is under stress. ... Members need to share a preconceived notion of what is correct behaviour, a 'business ethic, ' and think of it as a positive force, not a constraint. "The individual has a critical role in the development of the shared values.

Global Environment

Dealing with the ethics of employees, customers, and other stakeholders and the society from which they are drawn is a difficult task even in organizations that compete within a single domestic economy. However, the difficulty level increases for global organizations because value systems are highly divergent across international boundaries. For example, a survey of 3, 783 female seniors attending 561 universities and colleges in Tokyo revealed that they not only expected sexism in the workplace, but didn't seem to mind it. "More than 91 percent said they would not mind being treated as 'office flowers. 'Nearly 25 percent considered that to be a woman's role. Over 66 percent said acting like an office flower would make the atmosphere more pleasant.

"This attitude concerning the role of women, which is widely held in Japan, would be considered unacceptable in many other countries, including the United States. This clash of values is illustrative of the types of problems that exist across many international relationships. U. S. companies often experience cultural clashes when doing business with companies in China, Latin America, Russia, and many other countries. And, of course, firms from other countries often have difficulty understanding the values of Americans, Europeans, Australians, and so forth. The problem is a common one. The key to overcoming cultural clashes is working to understand the host-country culture and developing strategies that are consistent with that culture instead of fighting it.

Although there are dissimilarities among international cultures, it would be an overstatement to say that everything is different. In fact, as organizations grow, develop, and internationalize, they tend to adopt values that are friendlier to a wider group of international constituents. This is certainly true of hospitality companies.

Luiz Alberto Garcia, chairman of the board of directors of Algar, a large and successful Brazilian company with investments in a wide variety of service, agricultural, and manufacturing businesses. The statement was found at the beginning of Algar's recent annual report. Many of the elements of values, social responsibility, and enterprise strategy are included in the chairman's message. In fact, it could just as well have been the opening statement in the annual report of a U. S., European, or Asian company.

Algar is known today as being one of the most active companies in Brazil in terms of corporate citizenship as well as one of the best companies in which to work. We take great pride in such recognition. These are things that are part of our core values and beliefs. We have conducted training programs for our associates for many years now and our companies believe in-and invest in-actions of social responsibility. All of our relationships merge into an overall chain of action involving ethics, quality, commitment, and attitude. And believing in a better Brazil is also a business investment.

Bibliography

Horner, P. *Travel Agency Practice*, Longman: UK, 1996.

Horner, S. and Swarbrooke, J., *Marketing Tourism Hospitality and Leisure in Europe*, ITBP: UK, 1996.

Inkpen, G. *Information Technology for Travel and Tourism*, 2nd Longman: UK, 1998.

Ioannides, D. and Debbage, K.G. (eds), *The Economic Geography of the Tourist Industry: A Supply-Side Analysis*, Routledge: UK, 1998.

Johnson, P. and Thomas, B. (eds) *Perspectives on Tourism Policy*, Mansell: UK, 1992.

Jones, C. and Jowett, V., *Managing Facilities*, Butterworth Heinemann: UK, 1998.

Jones, P. and Kipps, M. (eds) *Flight Catering*, Longman: UK, 1995.

______________. and Lockwood, A., *The Management of Hotel Operations: An Innovative Approach to the Study of Hotel Management*, Cassell: UK, 1989.

______________. and Pizam, A. (eds), *The International Hospitality Industry: Organisational and Operational Issues*, Longman: UK, 1993.

______________, *Introduction to Hospitality Operations: An Indispensable Guide to the Industry*, Cassell: UK, 1996.

Kemp, K. and Pearson, S., *Leisure and Tourism: GNVQ Intermediate*, Addison Wesley Longman: UK, 1997.

Knowles, T., *Corporate Strategy for Hospitality*, Longman: UK, 1996.

______________. *Hospitality Management: An Introduction,* 2nd ed, Longman: UK, 1998.

Kotas, R. and Conlan, M., *Hospitality Accounting,* ITBP: UK, 1997.

Kotler, P., Bowen and Makens, *Marketing for Hospitality and Tourism,* Prentice Hall: UK, 1998.

Laws, E., *Tourism Marketing: Service and Quality Management Perspectives',* Stanley Thornes: UK, 1991.

______________. *Tourist Destination Management: Issues, Analysis and Policies,* ITBP: UK, 1995.

Lawson, F. *Hotels and Resorts: Planning, Design and Refurbishment,* Architectural Press: UK, 1995.

______________, *Tourism and Recreation Development,* Focal Press: UK, 1998.

Index